Mindfulness and Self-Regulation for Children

Over 70 Powerful Tasks + Workbook for Sensory Processing Disorder, ADHD, Trauma, and Anxiety

Vanessa B. McDonovan, Ph.D.

Table of Contents

Introduction 7
Chapter 1: What Is Mindfulness? 9
Chapter 2: Using This Book 12
Chapter 3: Mindful Exercises for Sensory Processing Disorder 14

Exercise 1: Five Breath Breathing 14
Exercise 2: Sword Breathing 16
Exercise 3: Weather Visualization 18
Exercise 4: Art Practice 20
Exercise 5: Squeezing Muscles 22
Exercise 6: Heartbeat Awareness 24
Exercise 7: Body Scanning 26
Exercise 8: Mindful Listening 28
Exercise 9: Bee Breathing 30
Exercise 10: STOP Mindfulness 32
Exercise 11: Box Breathing 34
Exercise 12: Rainbow Nature Walk 36
Exercise 13: Buddy Breathing Exercise 38
Exercise 14: Three Breath Hug 40
Exercise 15: Guided Body Moving Exercise 42
Exercise 16: Balancing on One Foot 43
Exercise 17: Mindful or Unmindful Worksheet 45
Exercise 18: The Present Moment Worksheet 46
Exercise 19: Starfish Meditation 47
Exercise 20: Meditations for Anger 49
Exercise 21: Pinwheel Breathing 50
Exercise 22: Child's Pose Yoga 52
Exercise 23: Downward Dog Yoga 54
Exercise 24: Blindfolded Taste Test 56
Exercise 25: The Feelings Thermometer 58

Chapter 4: Mindful Exercises for ADHD 60

Exercise 26: Personal Weather Report 60
Exercise 27: Drawing Your Breaths 62
Exercise 28: Mindful Snacking 65
Exercise 29: The Texture Bag 67
Exercise 30: Listening Mindfully to Music 69
Exercise 31: The Penny Game 71
Exercise 32: Melting or Freezing 73

Exercise 33: Mindful Hunting Game 75
Exercise 34: Mindful Simon Says... 77
Exercise 35: Mindful Nature Walk 79
Exercise 36: Mindful Red Light, Green Light 81
Exercise 37: Freeze Dance 83
Exercise 38: Shark Fin Breathing.. 85
Exercise 39: Breathing in Colors 87
Exercise 40: Sun Salutation Yoga Pose 89
Exercise 41: Feet Up Pose 91
Exercise 42: Mindful Swinging 93
Exercise 43: Watching Ripples 95
Exercise 44: Blowing Bubbles in Milk 97
Exercise 45: Mindful Cooking 99
Exercise 46: Wall Pushes.. 101
Exercise 47: Breathing and Tracing 103
Exercise 48: Feather Catching Game 104
Exercise 49: Follow the Maze 106
Exercise 50: Mindful Gardening... 108

Chapter 5: Mindful Exercises for Trauma and Anxiety 110

Exercise 51: The Glitter Jar.. 110
Exercise 52: Five Senses Grounding Exercise 112
Exercise 53: Roots to Rising Meditation... 114
Exercise 54: Gratitude Game 116
Exercise 55: Mindful Visualization 118
Exercise 56: Partner Breathing 120
Exercise 57: Mindful Barefoot Walking 122
Exercise 58: Superhero Senses 124
Exercise 59: Mindful Scavenger Hunt... 126
Exercise 60: The Silence Game... 128
Exercise 61: Anchoring 130
Exercise 62: Coloring Your Feelings 132
Exercise 63: Reframing a Thought 134
Exercise 64: Star Pose.. 135
Exercise 65: Make an I Spy Jar... 136
Exercise 66: Hand Full of Sand 138
Exercise 67: Mindful Guided Meditation 140
Exercise 68: Mindful Storytime.. 141
Exercise 69: Validating Emotions 143
Exercise 70: Sniffing Flowers and Blowing Candles 145
Exercise 71: Mountain Breath 147
Exercise 72: Pouring Paint.. 149
Exercise 73: Positive Thoughts and Affirmations 150

Exercise 74: Smile.. *151*
Exercise 75: Bubble Breathing... *153*

Conclusion **155**

Introduction

Congratulations on purchasing *Mindfulness and Self-Regulation for Children,* and thank you for doing so.

Mindfulness and self-regulation do not inherently go along with what people think that children are capable of. People usually assume that children are too young, too impulsive, and too unwilling or able to focus on being mindful or to self-regulate. How can they regulate themselves when they are so unlikely to stop and think things through? How can they make sure that they make the right decision when children are so incredibly impulsive?

Children, in general, tend to struggle with this impulsivity. However, impulsivity does not have to mean that your child cannot learn how to overcome it. It is possible to work with your children to discover the skills they will need to live mindfully and self-regulate. Especially for children that struggle with a sensory processing disorder, ADHD, have suffered from trauma, or are otherwise suffering from anxiety, being able to self-regulate is incredibly important.

When you can work with your children and teach them how to self-regulate, you teach them how to control themselves. You teach them how to work with themselves to develop a better coping method with their stress, anxiety, or feeling overwhelmed. You are giving them a gift of a lifetime, allowing them to focus on the moment, live in the moment, and ensure that they are doing what they need to do. You can help them learn how to recognize and accept their feelings. Because of that, you show that learning to control their emotions so they do not hurt other people or make bad decisions is entirely within the realm of possibility.

When your child learns to self-regulate and grow mindful, they are capable of great things. They earn how to stop and empathize with others. They learn how to recognize how their actions impact other people and how their feelings impact themselves. This gift of self-awareness will take your child far in life, and that is important.

This book is here to do that for you. It is here to introduce you to fostering mindfulness and self-regulation in children, whether those children are your own or children that you are around regularly. You will be given several different techniques that are meant to be fun, engaging, and exciting for young children to do, and they can be started as soon as your child is old enough to begin to follow directions. When you do these different tasks with the children around you, you will teach them to act in ways that will be good for them. You are teaching them to follow what they are supposed to do. You are giving them skills that they will need to live happy, successful lives and have happy, successful relationships. This book and its activities will help your child discover the best version of themselves that they can become.

Chapter 1: What Is Mindfulness?

Before we begin on the activities included in this book, we will first examine what mindfulness is. It is quite simple—to be mindful is to be entirely engrossed in the present moment. It is to look at the present without regard for anything else happening around you or worry about how other people will look at the situation. When you are mindful, you will find that you are entirely engrossed at the moment you are in. You are not distracted by anything else. You are intensely aware of what is happening right that second, and nothing else matters.

Mindfulness is a state in which you can recognize what is going on within you. It can see how you feel and understand what it means. It is being able to stop and recognize those feelings without letting them rule you at all. When you are mindful of what you are doing, you know how to regulate yourself out, powerful.

Likewise, when you teach your children to be mindful of their feelings and how their feelings impact them, your children learn how to understand what is going on within themselves. No matter the age, if your child is old enough to stop and listen to you when you speak to him or her, they are old enough to follow along with some of the most basic mindful exercises. By facilitating that degree of mindfulness in your child, you help them become gentle and accepting of the moment. They recognize that what is happening is happening, and there is no real way around it. This leads to a child that is less stressed inherently—they know that there is no way to fight what is happening around them, but they learn how to control their reactions to it.

Mindfulness helps minimize anxiety in children, and in doing so, inherently leads to more happiness as well. When a child is not constantly dwelling and worrying about what is happening, they are much more likely to be happy. They are going to find that they are successful in navigating the world around them.

Mindfulness becomes a useful skill for you to teach, then, to help eradicate that anxiety that could otherwise threaten to overwhelm your child. It can help your child learn to deal with their fears head-on and prevent themselves from feeling entirely incapable of coping with the world around them. A child that can work with mindfulness to help defeat that anxiety that comes to mind.

Children who struggle with sensory processing disorder may find that they struggle to cope with the stimuli all around them, and mindfulness can become a great tool for protecting them. With mindfulness, the attention can be shifted away from the stimuli that are becoming overwhelming and instead shift that focus elsewhere. Instead of, for example, focusing on the constant strain of loud noises that make it impossible to work without being distracted, you can teach your child to stop at the first sign of feeling overwhelmed, take some breaths or do something mindfully, and then move on.

Children with ADHD can also find these techniques greatly beneficial. With these techniques, children with ADHD can stop and refocus themselves when they need to. They can remind themselves of what they need to do and how they need to do it just by catching on to when they are starting to get overwhelmed. When they realize that they are jumping from focus to focus without paying attention to what they are doing, they will be capable of stopping themselves and regulating themselves out, just by learning to be mindful. Further, the mindfulness they will learn will teach them to be compassionate toward themselves when interacting.

These mindfulness methods can become incredibly beneficial to the children that learn to use them, and because of that, they should be fostered. The best way to foster mindfulness is to turn it into a lifestyle. The habits of mindfulness will create better behaviors for a happier lifestyle for the children that learn to live it, and all you have to do is implement these mindfulness exercises to encourage mindfulness, self-awareness, and self-regulation.

Chapter 2: Using This Book

Now, let's go over what to expect when you are using this book. Firstly, let go of the idea that mindfulness is nothing more than a tool. It is significantly more than that—it is a way of life, which is important to keep in mind. When you can live mindfully in a way that is entirely unencumbered by the distractions of the world, you can stay in the moment, and you can relieve a lot of the daily stressors that most people find themselves burdened with.

When you use this book, you are committing to teaching your child mindfulness, and the best way to do that, first and foremost, is to make sure that you are mindful of yourself. When you can maintain that mindfulness yourself, your child will naturally begin to pick up on it, which is important to remember.

Beyond just modeling this mindful living for your children, you will want to make these activities a major part of your routine. You will want to make sure that you are inserting chances for mindful living at every opportunity that you get because, in doing so, you will encourage and facilitate that success in your children. You can help them develop those skills by using these games and exercises designed to be engaging, exciting, and beneficial to the children who use them.

When using this book, keep in mind that this should not be a struggle. It should not be a battle. It should not be something that your children dread. If your children find that they dread these actions and behaviors, they are going to be miserable. They are going to resist using these methods because they will not matter to them. They will refuse to do the work willingly, and therefore, they will miss out on developing the skills that are meant to be used regularly.

Make sure that the use and development of mindfulness are fun. Take the stress and struggle out of the process altogether and help yourself to figure out exactly how you can, in fact, live life successfully and beneficially. Look at how you can facilitate enjoyment in these games and activities as if you can make your child believe that they are fun; your child will never feel like it is a struggle or a hassle to get through these processes. Your child will not be hindered or burdened by the idea that this is a chore, but rather, they will be encouraged to believe that mindfulness is something fun and enjoyable. They will develop their skills through sheer repetition, and they will want to continue to use these skills because they will find enjoyment in doing so.

Finally, as you are reading through this book, remember that you are your child's ultimate tool and guide. You are responsible for making sure that your child learns to do what he or she ultimately needs the most, and you can do that with these tools that are being provided to you. Remember to pick your battles wisely and allow your child to lead to some degree—it will help your child find enjoyment.

Chapter 3: Mindful Exercises for Sensory Processing Disorder

Exercise 1: Five Breath Breathing

The first exercise we are going to introduce is the five breath breathing exercise. This breathing exercise is designed to guide your child into centering him or herself, shaking off those overwhelming or anxiety-inducing emotions that may be currently running rampant in them. Breathing exercises are powerful. They keep the body regulated—after all, how could they not? Breathing is an integral part of life, and without it, you die. Breathing quickly can energize you, but taking big, deep breaths has the opposite effect. It can calm you and regulate your emotions.

When you are using this exercise, approach it as a game for your child. Your child will need to take five big, deep breaths with your guidance, and if you can make that happen, you can ensure that your child will be capable of calming themselves down.

To start, do the following:

1. Encourage your child to stop and look at you for a moment and instruct your child to take in a big, deep breath. They are going to take five big, deep breaths ultimately. Tell your child to focus on you, making eye contact with only you. The inhale should be through the nose

2. Encourage your child to then exhale deeply and slowly through the mouth. It has to be slow for the full calming effect while your child is looking at you.

3. Repeat this process while you slowly and gently count to five.

4. After the fifth breath, ask your child how they feel and what they notice is different.

When your child gets good at this activity, you can encourage your child to take five breaths with his or her eyes shut as well. This will allow your child to stop and pay attention by themselves so they can make use of this as a self-regulation method.

This process is relatively simple, but it encourages a mindful focus on the present and the current act of breathing. Your child may resist you at first—try not to be too discouraged if they do. Simply try again at another point. This is meant to be fun and engaging.

Remember that it is important to practice first with your child, happy and calm. You want to introduce those skills to be used and mastered until your child feels confident enough to use them when stressed out.

Exercise 2: Sword Breathing

The next exercise that we are going to consider is sword breathing. With this exercise, you will be guiding your child in taking deep breaths while also focusing on his or her body through hand movements. This will require your child to focus on their breath while synchronizing that awareness with their body movements. When this happens regularly, your child is mastering the art of mindfulness that is needed.

This is another example of breathing deeply and carefully to ensure that your child can do what they need most. When you are making use of this exercise, your child's deep breathing is triggering that calming reaction within him or her, and he or she is learning to focus intently on the act of breathing.

1. Start this exercise by encouraging your child to stop and take one big, deep breath through the nose and then let it all out slowly through the mouth.

2. Guide your child to turn his or her arm into a sword. You want your child to hold out their arm straight, with their wrists and elbows locked to make one straight line, and you want your child to make sure that fingers are lined up straight and the palm is flat.

3. Tell your child to raise their sword in the air when taking in a big, deep inhale. Your child should pull his or her arm up slowly as they breathe, moving the entire time that they continue to breathe in.

4. Tell your child to lower their sword as they exhale their breath out, encouraging them to move until they are done with the breath slowly.

5. Repeat this process at least five or six times.

Your child will have to focus on their breathing, their body, and their movements all at the same time, and that requires mindfulness and attention. Remember that this should be practiced as a game. You can turn it into other forms of imaginary swords that are not something that you are interested in promoting. Instead of a sword, you could encourage your child to gently and carefully move away vines with their walking stick if you are looking for something calmer.

Exercise 3: Weather Visualization

This next exercise encourages and focuses on your child's ability to understand their emotions. It can be hard for children to identify what they are feeling in the moment, and for that reason, you need to help them learn how they can express their emotions. By working on it with the weather as a sort of analogy, you can help your child begin to understand and facilitate those changes that they need to see in themselves.

You will be introducing your child to the idea of weather as emotions in this exercise. In essence, they will be visualizing themselves and their emotions like the weather around them, and that means that if they are struggling to tell you that they are feeling sad, they can then tell you that they are just feeling rainy or gloomy.

To start this exercise, you will need to do the following:

1. Create a weather chart with your child to help them understand the weather and the corresponding emotions that they may be feeling. You may find that you do this by superimposing certain faces atop certain types of weather. You may, for example, start by encouraging your child to associate sunny with happiness. Sadness will associate with rainy or cloudy. Grumpy could be a thunderstorm. You can have all of these different emotional states corresponding to weather, and your child will be able to begin figuring out how their emotions are by referring to them by the weather.

2. Encourage your child to talk about his or her emotions regularly with this weather chart. Tell them to figure out if what they are feeling is sunny

weather, rainy weather, cold weather, gloomy weather, or anything else.

3. Listen to your child when they talk to you about their weather report about their feelings any time they come to you.

4. When your child seems to be feeling something quite strongly, ask your child to report back about their weather report to get a better idea of what they are feeling in the moment.

When you do this, you are facilitating that self-awareness that is a necessary component of self-regulation. You are teaching your child to stop, think about his or her feelings, and then tell you how they feel so it can then be regulated well.

Exercise 4: Art Practice

Art practice is a great way to practice mindfulness. When you are drawing something or encouraging your child to draw something, there is plenty of focus on what is being done. You must be able to focus on what you are doing when you are drawing or coloring. You must be making deliberate movements and actions to ensure that you create the art you are looking to see. You can do this in many different ways.

When you encourage your child to practice their art, you encourage them to quietly and calmly create something new. You encourage them to watch what they are doing and focus entirely on the way they are moving. They must focus on their hands and how their hands are moving to create what they want. The best part about this activity too is that it is easy and fun for children! You do not have to do much at all—just tell your child to quietly color or draw a picture.

Watch your child when you do this—you should see them focusing entirely on their hand as they go, especially if they are younger. When this happens, your child is learning exactly how to focus entirely on their hand at the moment. Just about anything can be done mindfully, but art creates a tangible result that you can see.

1. Provide your child with plenty of art supplies and anything else that he or she may need. Encourage your child to be creative with what they are doing and tell them to create anything that comes to mind

2. Encourage your child to do anything they want, but make sure that they are quiet. It should be done in as much silence as possible. When you encourage this with your child, you make sure that your child can focus entirely on what is happening.

3. Set a timer for your child to remain quiet while doing their project and ensure that your child has everything needed.

4. Wait for the timer to go off, and then ask your child about what is being done. Ask what they are creating and how it is coming together. Allow your child to walk you through their drawing or art project and tell you what it is and why they like it.

This process will help your child tell you all about what they were doing, which requires mindfulness on its own. This requires your child to focus on what they have created and tell you why it matters in the first place. They can guide you through their art, and they practiced their ability to focus entirely on what they are doing in the first place.

Exercise 5: Squeezing Muscles

The next exercise is all about squeezing different muscles of the body. There are over 600 different muscles throughout the body, all working to keep your body working and give you the ability to move voluntarily. Some of these muscles are entirely voluntary, while others are automatic or involuntary, such as the heart. Can you focus on any particular muscle at any point in time?

Think about it—think about your left bicep for a moment. Are you suddenly acutely aware of it? Next, focus on your right quad. Are you suddenly aware of that instead? This is precise because you are capable of focusing on these body parts as they pop up. However, to do so, you must be focused on yourself. You must know how to hone and aim your focus to where it needs to go, and if you can do that, you are strengthening that mindful focus of yours.

This is what you will be encouraging your child to do. You will be guiding your child through how to identify every muscle they have in their body so they can then focus on it. You are trying to convince your child to focus their attention at very specific points and then encourage them to tighten them. This will be later when your child needs to tense and relax different areas of the body.

To do this, try turning it into a game of sorts. You call out something to tense up, and then your child has to do so. This can be a fun way to introduce your child to mindfulness while simultaneously introducing them to the idea of paying attention to their anatomy.

1. Start by encouraging your child to take in a big, deep breath. In doing so, you can then encourage your child to calm down. Maybe have your child do

a quick shake out if you are worried about them failing to focus on what they are guided to do in later steps. You can tell them to get their wiggles out if they are young and set a quick timer.

2. After the deep breath, call out a body part and tell your child to make it tight and tense. You want them to clench their muscle in that area that you call out. To verify that they are doing so right, you can then feel the muscle you have told them to tense.

3. Have your child hold the muscle nice and tight for a few moments before allowing them to let it go.

4. Repeat this process with several different muscles for as long as your child is interested in doing so. You can work with first calling out muscles by saying, "arm muscle" or "leg muscle," but eventually work up to calling out the proper muscles that are being moved if your child is old enough to do so.

5. Continue for a few moments until your child loses interest.

Exercise 6: Heartbeat Awareness

Next, we are going to spend some time focusing on the heartbeat and seeing how it changes. Many young children do not realize that their heart rate changes often. They do not pay attention to it—they are just busy going through their lives without paying attention. However, older children can be a bit more in tune with the idea.

When you are using this exercise, you will be encouraging your child to use their natural heartbeats. You want your child to see how it changes depending upon what they are doing to use that with a sense of mindfulness—you want them to see what they are doing and why it matters. When you do this, you will make sure that your child learns to pay closer attention to their body.

You will be encouraging your child to move around and then pay attention to the changes in heart rate. In doing so, you teach your child to reflect inwardly and pay attention to those quick little actions that are important. You will be able to do this in many different ways.

1. Encourage your child to stop and take a deep breath. Then, encourage your child to find their pulse, either on their chest or on their neck. Have them pay attention to it for some time.

2. Then, encourage your child to get up and run around. You can put on a timer and tell your child to run and jump or spin or do anything that will get their blood pumping. Have them do this for two minutes.

3. When the two minutes are up, encourage your child to stop and then return to feeling his or her pulse for a moment to see how it has changed through movement.

4. Encourage your child to stay in that position until their heartbeat settles down and returns to normal.

You can repeat this with all sorts of activities as well. For example, you could encourage your child to stop and feel their heart rate change as they took deep breaths. You could repeat this process by laying down or having them do this as they settle down for bed. You will teach your child to stop and pay attention to their heart rate and how their actions will directly influence it.

Exercise 7: Body Scanning

The next exercise that you can use with your children is known as body scanning. When you do this, you are essentially teaching your child how to stop and feel their entire body all around them. They will essentially be shifting their focus throughout their entire body to identify what they are feeling, why they feel it, and how they can relieve that tension. It is quite similar to playing the game with tensing muscles introduced previously.

The best way to teach your child to do this is to use a sort of guided meditation. You are essentially going to encourage your child to lie down, get comfortable, and then guide them through the process of identifying their entire bodies. Try something like reading the following script:

1. Get nice and comfy lying on your back. You want to let your arms and legs start to relax, and they should just lie flat next to you. Get comfortable and take a deep breath and close your eyes.

2. Take in a big deep breath through your nose. Feel how it flows through your chest. Feel your tummy moving up and down. The air comes in. Now, breathe out through your mouth. Feel the air moving out. Do this again... And again.

3. Now, start thinking about other parts of your body. Do you feel your feet? How do they feel right now? Are they cold? Do they want to move around? Are they sore from running? Are they tired? Keep feeling your feet right now. Breathe in.... And out...

4. Now think about your legs. How do your legs feel? Are they heavy and tired? Do they want to get up and run? Let them just relax in front of you and do not move. Do you feel your knees? What about your thighs? Take some more deep breaths in... And out...

5. Now, feel your tummy. It is moving up and down as you breathe. Can you feel inside your tummy? Is it hungry? Is it empty? Is it hurting? Do you feel something there? Are you sad? It's okay if you know that you feel something, but you don't know what it is... Just feel it a little bit longer.

6. Feel your chest. How is it moving as you breathe? Can you feel your heart? Do you feel a feeling in there? Focus on what you feel and let it happen.

7. Now feel your arms and hands. Do you feel how relaxed and heavy they are next to you? Keep breathing in... And out...

8. What about your head? How is your face or head feeling? Are you smiling? Are you sad? Are you feeling anything at all? Let it happen and enjoy it.

9. Now, pay attention to your whole body all at once. Take a big deep breath, and enjoy how you are feeling.

Exercise 8: Mindful Listening

Mindful listening is one of those skills that need to be learned over time. When you can listen mindfully, you know how to make sure that you are paying the attention that whatever you are listening to at that moment deserves. This is also a great introduction for children to begin to learn what it means to listen mindfully and a great introduction for mindfulness in general.

When your child tends to stress out about the world or get overwhelmed, it can help teach your child to stop and listen to just one particular thing at that moment. You teach your child that they need to pay attention to the world you are pointing at simply. You allow your child to focus on something to help them forget to be overwhelmed, powerful.

You can use just about anything to teach your child to listen mindfully. In this case, let's look at mindful listening with the chime of a bell. When you chime the bell, you know that what you are ultimately doing is ensuring that your child focuses on that one sound at the moment. They should pay attention to it the entire time that it rings until it fades out. Try doing the following:

1. Get a bell, a gong, a chime, or anything else that will ring out for a while. You could also use a piano or a guitar or other string instrument in a pinch—you just want to ensure that the sound will ring for a while.

2. Tell your child that it is time to listen to the bell and focus on it. Encourage your child to do so carefully and comfortably. Remind your child to remain nice and still while the bell rings and encourage your child to focus on it.

3. Tell your child to take a nice, big, deep breath for a moment and to close his or her eyes. Remind your child of the rule—no opening eyes until the sound has faded entirely.

4. Ring the bell and let it ring for a while. Allow it to fade into nothingness and watch as your child listens.

5. After the bell stops, encourage your child to open their eyes and then ask how your child feels after that. Ask how hard it was to listen. Ask if your child got distracted. Ask how it felt to sit still and listen.

Exercise 9: Bee Breathing

Bee breathing is a technique that is commonly used by people in yoga. It is supposed to make people feel relaxed and centered when they do it. It encourages a new kind of focus on breathing around you—a kind of breathing that is different and purposeful. Instead of simply breathing in and out to allow that breath to calm you, you use that breath to ensure that you can make sure that your child is learning to clear his or her mind. It can help to drown out sensory overload as well, making it perfect for trying if your little one has SPD.

This process can be taught to your child as a game. You can tell your child that they listen for the little bees around them when they do this. Remember, as always; you want to practice and solidify these methods when your child is in an agreeable mood rather than when he or she is frustrated or annoyed with what is happening. When you turn it into a game that can be practiced over time, you allow your child to begin to focus on what is happening. Your child will learn how to focus their breathing so they can begin to clear their mind. Try walking your child through the following steps:

1. Start by making sure that you are comfortable where you are sitting or lying down. You can sit, or you can lie down; however, you prefer.

2. Feel your shoulders begin to relax. Feel them droop lower and lower into the ground like they are sinking into the earth. Let them move down and back, but don't move them yourself. Close your eyes, and just breathe for a moment. Don't you feel relaxed?

3. Keep your mouth shut and breathe in through your nose—make it a big, deep breath and put your

hands over your ears. Then, make the sound of the letter M as long as you can.

4. Make the M sound as long as possible. Don't you hear the bees? Do it again. And again. Keep your eyes closed and keep buzzing for as long as it feels good.

5. When you are done buzzing like a bee, it is time for you to stop. Take a big, deep breath and let it go. Do you feel better now?

Exercise 10: STOP Mindfulness

For children who do not know how to manage themselves when the stress starts to pick up, one of the best activities you can try to with them is to help them learn how to stop and STOP. STOP here stands for Stop, Take, Observe, Proceed.

You will encourage your child to simply stop for a moment and learn how to mindfully be in the moment, no matter how stressed out they were just moments prior. The best way to introduce this practice is through gameplay. It could become a mindful game of red light green light in which when you tell your child to stop, they must go through all of the steps. Encourage your child to use this method when they need to ensure that they can manage their emotions at the moment. You will do the following with your child:

1. First, you must stop. This is the first step in the process. Your child must completely stop and look at you for the moment. They must be as still as they can at this point.

2. Take a few big, deep breaths now. Encourage your child to breathe in through the nose and then out through the mouth, just as he or she has been doing in other exercises.

3. Now, it is time to observe. What are you feeling right at that moment? How are you feeling? Acting? What are your thoughts? Are those emotions being shown elsewhere? Is your body acting happy or angry?

4. Finally, it is time to proceed—you need to choose to do something that will help you. If you are feeling overwhelmed, how can you make that feeling go

away? How can you make sure that you start to feel better so you do not get upset? What is going to make you feel good right now?

5. With the exercise done, talk to your child about keeping them on track and doing what they need to stay happy.

Exercise 11: Box Breathing

The next exercise is one inbox breathing. This may sound kind of strange, but all it is doing is encouraging your child to breathe deeply while following a box-like cycle. You can draw a big box for your child and have them trace the one you have made or use it. All that matters here is that you and your child have that square shape for you and the reminder on how to breathe with it to make it work for you. When you do this well, you will find that your child will learn to use these steps calmly and regularly, and eventually, may not even need the square shape at all—they will just be able to visualize it.

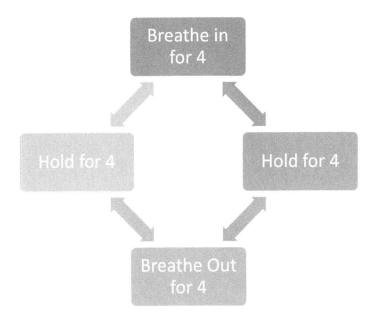

1. Start by looking at the square. Notice how it goes in for four seconds, holds for four seconds, goes out for four seconds, and then hold for four seconds. This is a square breathing exercise because it is the same at every step that you are following.

2. Now, put your finger on the corner that says to breathe in. Take in a big deep breath for four seconds.

3. Now, move your finger to the next corner and hold it for four seconds. You can do it!

4. Move your finger down and then breathe it out slowly and gently for four seconds

5. And now go to the next corner and hold it for four seconds.

6. Keep repeating this until you are feeling better.

Exercise 12: Rainbow Nature Walk

This next exercise is less about making sure that you and your child can follow steps and take your child out into the world to explore mindfully. Children are naturally quite mindful—if you have ever watched your son or daughter get entirely lost in a book, game, art, or anything else, you know this. You know that children can be hard to pull away when they have their minds locked on something, and because of that, you must learn how you can make sure that you can facilitate this. It is not stubbornness or ignoring you—it is mindfulness at its finest.

The next time that you have some good weather consider fostering that sort of mindfulness. If you have a tween or an early teen, you may find that they are entirely reluctant to do this, but if you have a younger child, you may be surprised to realize that your child naturally wants to do what you want them to do. Your child wants you to be happy. Your child wants to spend time with you, which is one of the greatest ways to do so.

Take your child out on a walk. Ensure that you do not have phones, or if you must carry your phone, it is on silent. No tablets, no distractions. You and your child must walk through the trail you are taking—it could be a city walk, a park walks, or even hiking. Where you go does not matter so much so long as you pay attention to your surroundings.

Make it a game. The first person to find the whole rainbow of living things is the winner. This means that each person must find something red, orange, yellow, green, blue, indigo, and violet, and there can be no repeats. Make sure that, aside from pointing out what you see, this walk is entirely silent. You and your child want to focus on the world around each other, not the conversation that you are having.

Exercise 13: Buddy Breathing Exercise

Especially if you have a younger child that struggles with self-regulation, you may find that encouraging your child to take in those big, calming deep breaths is next to impossible. When that happens, it is important to remember that you can ultimately make sure that your children can do these deep breathing exercises. All you have to do is make sure that you can engage your child to make them eager to follow along rather than entirely uninterested in doing so.

One way to do so with younger children and breathing is to introduce them to buddy breathing. When you introduce buddy breathing, you provide them with a breathing exercise that you know will help them. You are allowing them to see that they can have fun with these mindfulness exercises at the end of the day. To use buddy breathing, all you have to do is make sure that you teach your child to breathe with a stuffed animal or another toy to be their buddy.

1. Encourage your child to choose a breathing buddy. Keep in mind that it will be on their stomachs, so you want to choose something light that will not be too heavy or uncomfortable. When they choose it, point out that the buddy is quite angry or upset at the moment and needs help.

2. Then, encourage your child to put the buddy on their tummy while lying flat on their back. Encourage a quick breath and point out how the belly buddy moves with them and how that is a great way to encourage your child to keep breathing deeply and regularly.

3. Encourage one big deep breath and point out how the belly buddy moves up higher and higher.

4. Then, exhale, and watch while the buddy goes down lower and lower.

5. Encourage your child to repeat this and remind your child of why this works so well. Tell your child that when they do this, they can feel better and more in control of their emotions, and that is something that they can do on their own without needing help.

6. Point out that breathing buddy is feeling much calmer now after that ride, and then allow your child to remain in this position for as long as they are entirely comfortable.

Exercise 14: Three Breath Hug

The next exercise that you are going to do is use the three breath hug. When you encourage and facilitate this, you make sure that you are giving your child a few quick moments to sit and relax in your arms, and sometimes, that can make all the difference when your child is getting overwhelmed and feels like he or she cannot cope any longer. When you do this particular exercise, you are making sure that your child recognizes that you are there and present with him or her and helping them feel better. The trick, however, is making sure that you are mindful and present during the entire process.

1. Start by taking in a big, deep breath. Ask your child to take in a big deep breath with you. Allow your child to see you breathing in deeply as he or she breathes in deeply. You will be synchronizing your breathing, so make sure that you are taking breaths the size that your child can realistically and reasonably sustain for the moment.

2. Then, ask your child to come closer for a hug. Ask your child to come as close as possible and then hug tight; make sure that your child feels your chest against his or hers, and you do the same for them. Take in that big, deep breath again with them. In... and out...

3. Do this again, feeling each other's chests pressing against each other as you do so. Do you feel each other's pulse? Can you recognize the movements of the other person? Pay close attention to the feeling of your child and feel them melt into you.

4. Finally, take one more big, deep breath together and then let yourselves relax.

5. Ask your child how they feel after having completed that hug—did it help with the anger and frustration? Did it leave him or her feeling entirely relaxed? Were they happy? How are they feeling now?

This method is a great one to use before bed as well. Hugging is great to create all of those relaxation hormones that will help your little one start winding down more and more.

Exercise 15: Guided Body Moving Exercise

Next, you will take a look at an exercise that will get you and your child up, on your feet, and moving around. You are essentially going to be guiding your child through movements, describing what you want them to do to get them to stop, focus on their listening and also focus on their moving to make sure that you and your child are in perfect sync with each other.

When your child tends to get overwhelmed or struggles with the world, sometimes, it helps to turn that attention inward, and that is exactly what you are going to be doing with this. You will be reminding yourself and your child what you will need to do to move one's body to help self-regulate mindfully.

1. Start by encouraging your child to stretch and get ready. Tell them to take in a big, deep breath before beginning to help them feel nice and ready for the fun. Allow them to feel better as you do so—remind them that they are doing this for fun right now.

2. Ask your child to move—any movement. Maybe you ask them to slowly and gently raise their hands to the sky like a tree. Maybe they are going to sway in the wind. Maybe they are going to do just about anything else. It does not matter what you choose to have your child do—just encourage them to do so.

3. Keep having your child move gently or not so gently if you prefer. It does not matter, so long as you and your child are both happy with the result. You and your child should feel like you both can continue to exercise and have a good time.

Exercise 16: Balancing on One Foot

Did you know that standing on one foot takes a lot of focus? You may not realize it so much anymore now that you are older, but learning to make this happen and then executing it properly is hard work. When you encourage your child to do this, they will have to stop and focus on their balance. They will need to find that center of gravity, how to tap into it and how to ensure that at the end of the day, they can make sure that they are moving themselves and their bodies in a way that is going to help them rather than make things harder.

When they are currently frustrated or upset, encouraging your child to stop and balance on one foot can be fun and mindful and a great way to distract from those bad feelings in the first place. When you encourage this action, you allow them to stop and pay attention to themselves in a way that they may never have thought to do before. If you want to make it harder, you can add extra steps to the process as well—you could encourage your child, for example, to stop and hold both arms out like an airplane during this. You could tell your child to balance a ball on their hand, which may alter that center of gravity just enough to make them have to focus more.

1. Start by telling your child to take a big, deep breath and stretch their arms up toward the sky, as high as they can reach. Let their breath exhale out.

2. Then, encourage your child to lift their foot with their next inhale, slowly pulling it up while arms stay up toward the sky.

3. Try adding extra steps to the process—ask your child to make their arms move like a flamingo. Ask them

to pretend their arm is an elephant trunk and that they need to sound their trumpets. No matter what you choose to encourage, make sure that they can do it and happily go along with it because they know that it will make them feel better.

4. Add extra challenges to the mix—come up with new poses to do on one foot.

5. Finish up and take a big, deep breath, and then let your child move on with his or her day.

Exercise 17: Mindful or Unmindful Worksheet

This exercise is all about identifying mindful actions and unmindful actions. Print this page out and have your child circle the mindful actions for you. If your child is too young to read or you cannot print it out, you can also read out the sentences and then ask your child to identify whether they are mindful or not.

Forgetting to pick up your shoes when you get home from school

Helping someone pick up something that they have dropped

Yelling loudly when you see someone reading a book

Not turning on the light when your sister is sleeping

Pulling the dog's tail because it looks fun

Working on a new skill that you want to get better at

Exercise 18: The Present Moment Worksheet

This next worksheet that can be printed out is all about how to identify the present moment. You are essentially encouraging your child to stop and focus at the moment. You are having your child focus on that present moment and identify what is there.

As with before, if your child cannot read or your child is not comfortable writing, you can do this verbally as well.

Right now, I can see...

Right now, I can hear....

Right now, I can touch...

Right now, I can smell...

Right now, I feel...

Exercise 19: Starfish Meditation

This next meditation can be quite fun with young children. Essentially, you teach your child to stop and focus, not only on their breathing but also on themselves and their hands. You are encouraging them to breathe, to watch, and to trace, all at once, and especially for younger children, that will require a lot of focus.

When you use this meditation, all you need is your child, a flat surface, and your child's hand. It is that simple. All you are going to do is guide your child through tracing his or her hand to help them identify how they are feeling, why it matters, and how to be present at the moment. When you do this with your child, you are helping them develop that tend to be the best they can be, and if you do it right, you will ensure that your child is capable of calming down.

1. Start by encouraging your child to pay attention to their hand. Tell them to take it, spread it out, and plant it flatly on the table in front of them. They want to spread out all of their little fingers and imagine that it is a starfish in front of them.

2. The starfish is quite stressed out right now and needs help relaxing. The best way that the starfish feel better is through taking big, deep breaths and being rubbed along the sides and front; you tell your child. You encourage your child to do this carefully and quietly.

3. Watch as your child takes a big, deep breath and traces their hand, starting from one end by the wrist, tracing up the fingers, down the fingers, back up again and down again until they have gone through the whole and arrived at the other side.

4. Encourage your child to do this again as well, reminding them that the starfish is still stressed out and the starfish still needs help relaxing.

5. Repeat this until you see your child start to calm down as well.

Exercise 20: Meditations for Anger

Sometimes, you need to help your child stop and self-reflect to eliminate that anger and help them discover themselves, their passion, and everything they need. The best way to make this happen is through playing a guided meditation to help them begin to focus on that anger, how to melt it away, and how to recognize it for what it is—something that should not be ignored or neglected.

When you want to use these methods, make sure you are taking the time to encourage your child to sit and listen. You may choose to do so by making sure that meditation will be interesting to them. You may find a video online, for example, that will help you by reading the meditation for your child in the first place.

Exercise 21: Pinwheel Breathing

Children love pinwheels, especially when they are younger. They like to watch the pinwheels spin all around them, and they like to make it happen themselves. They take big, deep breaths to blow on the pinwheels to watch what happens. Sometimes, they like to take slow, soft breaths to see what happens, too. They do this to see exactly what is going to happen with their pinwheels. It is a trial and error thing where they want to see how they can interfere with the world and what will happen when trying something new.

You can facilitate and foster this as well quite simply. All you have to do is make sure that you give your child what they need—a pinwheel and a chance to experiment. With that, anything could happen.

1. Start by giving your child a pinwheel and make sure that you have one yourself as well. They can be

colorful, or they can be plain—it doesn't matter. Let your child pick one that seems to resonate with him or her.

2. Now, take in a big long breath and encourage your child to do the same. Breathe out together, using a long, deep breath, watching what happens with the pinwheel when you do so. What does it do? How does the pinwheel move?

3. Ask your child how he or she feels after doing that. Are they feeling good or tired? Do they feel happy or angry? Are they pleased to be doing what they are doing, or are they ready to stop?

4. Now, take a few quick short breaths and puff them at the pinwheel. Do this with your child, encouraging your child to do the same. How does he or she feel now? Energized? Ready to keep going?

5. Now, take a normal breath and let your normal breath out on the pinwheel, guiding your child through doing so as well

At the end of doing this, you can stop and ask your child how they feel. Ensure that your child is picking up that the different breaths lead to different feelings within him or her. Point out how the long slow breaths are designed to slow the body while the short, fast ones are energizing.

Exercise 22: Child's Pose Yoga

Another great way to make mindfulness happen is by encouraging your child to make sure that they know how to move. Yoga is great for this—with different movements, you can make yourself feel calm or make yourself feel energetic and alive. You can make yourself feel capable of anything at all, and you can make yourself want to take a nap.

One such pose that will help this happen is the child's pose in yoga. Thankfully, teaching your child yoga is not too difficult. Children love to move, and this, in particular, is a pose that children seem to gravitate toward in the first place. This is the perfect way to help your child figure out how to move, self-regulate, and ensure that he or she will be able to be successful at attempting to calm down.

1. Start by encouraging your child to kneel on the floor. Knees and big toes should be touching each other at this point.

2. Now, sit back on the heels of your feet. As you do this, your knees should start to separate. Knees need to be hip-width apart for proper effect.

3. Next, lower your head, slowly and gently, so you do not bump it. Rest it on the floor, and allow yourself to relax.

4. Let your hands and arms rest comfortably next to you on the floor

5. Relax and breathe.

Your child can stay in this pose for however long that he or she wants to. Over time, he or she will find that calmness will take over. This is an inherently calming pose—it stretches out the chest, opens up and broadens the shoulders, and makes sure that the whole body feels good.

Exercise 23: Downward Dog Yoga

Another common yoga poses for children is the downward dog pose. This is quite simple to teach, as well. It will help your antsy child stretch and feel better about him or herself. They will be able to clear their minds and able to focus and recognize what it is that he or she needs at any time better. All you will have to do is guide your children through some quick and simple steps.

You may even find that your child already does these poses quite often on his or her own, and that is okay, too. This movement requires balance, and balance requires mindfulness, so any uses of these methods will be good. Your child will not only start to feel better, but they will also help strengthen their spine, stretch out their muscles, and begin to relax.

1. Start by getting on hands and knees. Your wrists should be underneath your shoulders, and make sure that your knees are right under your hips. You are kind of like a table right now with four straight legs.

2. Press the balls of the feet into the floor like you are going to stand up. Let your bottom move up toward the ceiling. As you do this, make sure that your knees come off of the ground and straighten out.

3. Stretch your back as much as you can, slowly and gently. It should not hurt—it should feel good and fun.

4. Stay in this pose. Your feet are probably not quite touching the ground. Your toes are on the ground, but your heels do not quite reach, and that is okay.

Stay here for a while, and think about your feet touching the floor.

5. Stay in this pose for a while, and then bend your knees to stop it. Let your knees fall to the ground and take a big deep breath. Now, you can go into a child's pose as well if you want to do so.

Exercise 24: Blindfolded Taste Test

The next activity to try is the blindfolded taste test. When you do this, you are encouraging your child to try out several foods without being able to see what they are in front of them. You will give them bites of food on a fork, and they will then have to figure out what the food is, thinking about it.

When your child does this, they have to focus on that sense of taste as much as they can. They do this to try to figure out what it is that they have been fed, and you can have fun watching. They have to focus and practice, and you find that you can enjoy your time with your child. You can even take turns, where you get a blindfold, and your child gives you foods, too!

1. Start by blindfolding your child and then coming up with a series of snacks that can be given in quick, easy bites. Ensure that the foods you are giving are somewhat familiar, so your child does not feel like they are entirely lost with what is being given. You want them to feel like the food is something they know, even if they cannot place it the first time.

2. Give your child a bite of the food and begin to ask your child questions about what is being eaten. You may ask them what it tastes like and how it feels on the tongue, whether sweet or salty, or sour or bitter. You can ask them if it is spicy or if it is bland or has a strange texture. Is it mushy? Is it crunchy? What is it?

3. Your child will guess the food, and you let him or her know whether they are right.

4. Then, repeat this with another food, and then another.

5. Try to repeat this at least four or five times to encourage that mindfulness and make sure that your child can stop and focus on it.

You should find that, over time, your child gets good at this sort of mindful eating. They will be able to taste the difference between their foods far better than you expected them to do so—and that's great! It means that they are doing what they are supposed to do, and they are learning those skills that you are trying to instill in them.

Exercise 25: The Feelings Thermometer

Some kids feel like their emotions get the best of them. This is only natural—feelings get the best of everyone at some point or another, which is okay. However, your child must learn that they need to figure out how to regulate their own emotions, and for that, they have their feelings thermometer.

This is most often used for anger or other intense feelings that will be intense and potentially even destructive. You will want to make sure that you draw out a thermometer for your child and divide it up. You will have low, medium, and high. This will sort of rank how your child is feeling at any moment.

On one side of the thermometer, write what your child does when the feelings are intense. You may have that when your child is very angry, they yell or they hit. When they are sort of angry, they get louder, and they glare and make mean faces. When they are a little annoyed, they may groan and growl about it.

On the other side of the thermometer, you want to write down what your child can do when they get to those points. When your child is so angry that he or she wants to hit, for example, you may encourage your child to go and take a quick time out in his or her room. When he or she is somewhat angry, there are deep breaths used. When they are a little bit angry, you encourage some other action that distracts the anger.

When you use this thermometer idea with your child, you should put it up with your child somewhere that they can see readily. When you notice your child getting angry, you then ask them how hot their anger is and point to the thermometer. Your child should then stop and go to find how hot or not their feelings are at that moment, allowing you to see what they are feeling while also helping your child figure out their emotions at the moment to help them.

Chapter 4: Mindful Exercises for ADHD

Exercise 26: Personal Weather Report

This exercise is teaching your child how to report their internal weather. This is stemming from the weather visualization exercise that was introduced earlier within this book. When you use this with your child, you are encouraging your child to extrapolate from other activities. You teach your child how to stop and pay attention to their inner weather to report what they feel to you.

You can do this by having your child do a morning, afternoon, and evening weather report for their feelings for the day. Ensure that your child takes a little bit of time each morning, afternoon, and evening to write down their feelings in the form of weather, whether through drawing a picture for those children that are still too young to write or through actually writing down their feelings.

Try having your child do the following:

1. Create a picture showing their feeling about the weather of their emotions in the morning, afternoon, and evening. Talk about how the weather and the textures go together, and practice naming the feelings with their names rather than weather to encourage emotional self-awareness.

2. Create a forecast for the next day's expected weather as well, writing down what your child would like to see themselves feeling the next day. Encourage them to predict this based on what their schedule for the day is, if applicable.

3. Every day, compare the day's weather report to the previous day's forecast and see how accurate they are. Encourage your child not to worry about whether their emotions are right or wrong—emphasize just being able to recognize and name them in the first place.

4. Open a dialogue about the weather of the day and help your child learn how to make the necessary connections when talking about it.

Exercise 27: Drawing Your Breaths

This next exercise is all about drawing your breaths—literally. You will be guiding your child to pay attention to their breathing and create literal representations of their breathing on the paper for themselves to see and explore. You can encourage them to explore their breathing in different patterns—what does it look like when they breathe quicker or slower? There is no right or wrong way to do this, so get as creative as you and your child would like.

All you need for this is a sheet of paper of some sort and then whatever the chosen medium is. It could be crayons, markers, paint, or just about anything else you would like to use. Gather up your materials and then guide your child through the following steps.

When you use this exercise with your children, you are encouraging them to stop and become self-aware. You are guiding them through focusing as much as they can specifically on their breathing. You are honing their focus, even if only for a moment, and that can be a powerful skill to teach your child.

1. Gather up all of the desired supplies. You can ask your child what they want to use in particular or make your own decision.

2. Tell your child to take a crayon, pencil, marker, or whatever another drawing medium is being used and a piece of paper. Spend a few moments encouraging your child to stop and breathe—and feel it. No alterations have to be made here. They can breathe as quickly or as slowly as they are naturally. All that matters is that for now, all they need to do is breathe and pay attention to it.

3. After a minute of paying attention to the breathing, tell your child to put the tip of their drawing medium down on the paper and begin. They can draw however they want—there is no right or wrong way to do so. Some people will draw with a straight line as they breathe, and then wiggling, wavy lines as they breathe out. Others will do big, sweeping circles around the paper as they breathe in. Allow your child to do anything they want, so long as it is to the rhythm of their breathing.

4. Encourage your child to focus on their breathing and then change it up. Tell your child to take quick breaths instead of slow ones while drawing them for a moment, perhaps on a different sheet of paper. Then, try the same with slower breaths as well.

5. Compare the drawings on different pages. How do they vary? What does your child notice?

6. Ask how your child feels after completing this activity in the first place.

Exercise 28: Mindful Snacking

Children are continually eating and snacking. This makes sense—their stomachs are generally quite small, yet they need plenty of food to ensure that they are getting the nutrition they need. However, often, eating is mindless and distracted. This exercise will bring mindfulness to the eating scene to help your child learn how to eat something to encourage that mindful activity better mindfully.

You can do this with just about any snack or just about any meal—all that matters is that your child will be paying perfect attention to what they are eating. You want their complete focus on the food in their mouths so they can work on that sort of mindfulness in the first place.

1. Begin by placing some food on the table for your child. This could be their next meal or a handful of different snacks on a plate. This can work best with several different foods of different textures to allow your child to explore them.

2. Encourage your child to take a single, slow bite and tell them to focus on the food. They want to pay attention to how the food feels in their mouths. How does it feel on the tongue? Does it melt and flow? Is it solid? Hard? Soft? Chunky or smooth? What does it taste like? Is it sweet or sour? What does it remind your child of?

3. Guide your child to carefully and mindfully consider every bite of food, thinking about what it is and how it feels in their mouths, and then encourage them to talk about their observations.

Now, this is an excellent practice for just about anyone. Still, if you are worried about your child spending far too long eating during this process at a meal, you can alter it to involve the first few bites being mindful before you revert to a regular mealtime without the added mindfulness.

Exercise 29: The Texture Bag

This exercise is all about encouraging your child to focus on what they can feel when they are blind to something. It will teach your child to focus entirely on what they are touching within a bag that they cannot see into. It is meant to facilitate more of that same self-awareness and the moment attitude explored with the last few activities. This activity is all about making sure that your child can stop and focus on what is in front of them, even if only briefly.

To build your bags, just about anything safe for children to touch is a fair game. You will be taking a paper bag, like from a grocery store or like the ones that children often will use for their school lunches, and filling it up with different textures. You may, for example, fill it up with sand or rice. You may fill it up with dry noodles or marbles. You could even fill it with a mix of several different things and encourage your child to figure out what is inside it; if you want to use wet objects or something that you would worry about leaking through the paper bag, try to line the inside of the bag with a plastic bag and taped inside to contain the mess.

Once you have your bag all set up, go through the following steps:

1. Give your child the textured bag and encourage them not to look inside of it. Explain that they will feel inside and have to guess what it is without them peeking in it. This turns it into a sort of game for your child and encourages them to want to continue.

2. Let your child reach into the bag without looking and without pulling anything out of the pocket. Your child is going to be considering what is inside of the bag without ever looking. Ask what they feel and what they notice about what is in there.

3. Spend several minutes exploring various bags filled with different materials and textures to figure out and make sure that your child tells you what they think is inside to compare later on.

4. When you are done, show your child what was inside each bag to guess what it was. Were they right or wrong? Are they surprised?

Exercise 30: Listening Mindfully to Music

This next exercise encourages your child to sit and listen to a song, focusing on what they hear and every instrument. You may find that the best way to make this happen for your child is by encouraging them to follow just one instrument at a time as they listen, learning to focus entirely on it as they follow along.

At first, especially if your child struggles to focus for very long, you may find that the best way to make sure that your child feels successful is to either use a concise song or even just use a single verse of the song that you are encouraging them to listen to. This can slowly be lengthened out as your child learns how to focus more in the future.

1. Choose out a song, or a portion of a song, that you would like to guide your child. Allow them to listen to the song once to hear how the whole thing sounds.

2. Tell your child to sit down and close their eyes for a moment. Then, encourage them to listen to just one instrument within the song as it plays. Ask them to feel the music in their bodies as they do with their eyes closed.

3. Watch as your child focuses on the music. You may notice them tapping, moving, or swaying to the beat of the music, and that is okay. So long as they are focusing on the music, that is okay. All that matters is that you encourage them to concentrate to some degree.

4. When the song ends, ask how the music made them feel. Was it exciting and bouncy? Did it make them feel sleepy and relaxed? Was it full of energy?

5. Play the music again and ask your child to pay attention to another part instead.

6. Repeat this as often or as little as you want, focusing on the different instruments, voices, and just about anything else within it.

Exercise 31: The Penny Game

This is a fun game that you can play with your child or children to learn how to focus on an object's details. If you have  more than one child, they can all play this game together, adding an extra layer of challenge to the mix. Your child is supposed to sit and pay attention to precisely what their penny looks like and then toss it back into a bunch with several other pennies. Then, your child will have to figure out which one is his or hers. This will allow them to stop and pay attention to what they have in their hands, and that helps them build up the ability to figure out what they were holding in the first place.

When you use this method, you encourage and foster that attention to detail that mindfulness entails, and that is important. Guide your child through the following steps:

1. Take a roll of pennies and dump them onto a table. You can use fewer pennies if you want to make this easier for a younger child.

2. Ask your child to pick out a penny of their own. Encourage them to look at the penny very, very carefully.

3. Give your child one minute to carefully look at their pennies, paying close attention to the details.

4. When the minute is up, take the penny, put it back into the group, and mix it up. Then, ask your child to find their penny.

5. When they do find their penny, ask how they know it was theirs.

Exercise 32: Melting or Freezing

This next exercise is all about encouraging your child to recognize their emotions and work to melt them away. When we are stressed out, sad, scared, or anything else, it is entirely possible for you to sort of freeze-up—you cannot help it, but it happens. You then find that you are wholly stuck in yourself for some time. Many children can feel like their minds are frozen when they feel any sort of strong feelings, which is a problem for them—they wind up feeling stuck. They feel like it is impossible to think during this period.

However, you can help your child learn to stop doing this—they can allow themselves to thaw and melt instead of being stuck in a freeze. When that happens, they learn to release all of that negativity away to get back to themselves. Practice freezing and melting before your child needs it to be sure that they can do this well independently.

1. Start by telling your child to be like a snowman for a moment. Ask them to feel like they are frozen like a snowman. Ask them if they know what it would be like to be a snowman. They may stand with their arms up and out like a snowman would, for example. Remind them to be tense and frozen.

2. Spend a moment being a snowman and then ask them what happens to snowmen when they get warm. Your child will most likely answer that they melt. Then, guide your child through melting like a snowman. Describe the sun on them, slowly making themselves start to meltdown. Maybe their head gets warm first and starts to move around. Then the

shoulders, and their tummies and backs, then their legs, too. Guide them through imagining that they are slowly melting away into a puddle on the ground.

3. Allow them to spend some time relaxing on the ground, entirely melted away into the puddle, and then ask your children what they feel like now. Let them stay there for a moment and then encourage them to stand up big and tall like people again.

4. Ask them what a melting snowman was like, and then ask them how they feel after thawing.

Exercise 33: Mindful Hunting Game

Children love to play games. They like to pretend that they are off adventuring and doing different things, no different. When you play this game, you encourage your child to stop, listen, and pay attention to the world around them. You will be supporting a moment of mindfulness in which your child is aware of everything without focusing on anything at all. This is an important skill to develop—when your child can do this, they can begin to focus.

You could do this just about anywhere—outside, inside, or even in a car if you needed to. All that matters is that you and your child will be stopping to hunt for something—it may be something that you can find quite easily, or it may be harder. For the first time that you pay this, you may try doing it somewhere relatively quiet.

1. Encourage your child to go outside into your back yard, if you have one, or take your child to the park if you do not. Go far away from everyone else and tell your child that you are doing something extraordinary—you are hunting.

2. You need to explain to your child that you need to remain beautiful, quiet, and still. You are listening very carefully because you are hunting for something. You can make up what you are tracking or ask your child to make up something instead. All that matters is that you and your child will stop and listen.

3. With your target in mind, stop, be still, and focus all around you, looking for what you are hunting. For example, if you want to hunt a squirrel, you may decide to spend some time with all ears open,

paying attention to the world around you to listen for the rustling of grass or leaves. If you are hunting for a bee, you may listen for a buzz. No matter what you are listening for, however, you will need to focus.

4. See if your child can practice this sort of stillness as well, encouraging them not to get distracted. Sometimes, having that extra goal to aim for can help them develop that focus that they are ultimately looking for.

Exercise 34: Mindful Simon Says

Children are great at games, and they are often some of the best ways to encourage your child to learn a lesson. When you make learning fun, it is hardly a chore. In this game, you will be teaching mindfulness to encourage playing, movement, and engagement.

This is just like the traditional game of Simon Says— however, in playing this game, the instructor also needs to show the behavior as well. Sometimes, Simon can put in distracting behavior, choosing to do the opposite of the command given. Sometimes, there is no, "Simon says," at the beginning of the command, meaning that there is no action. You can play this alone with your child, or you can do it in a group as well. You will do the following:

1. Choose a leader for the game. The leader will be giving commands with the form of "Simon says…" Everyone has to follow along. With each command given, the leader must also display the behavior themselves as well. For example, "Simon says, jump up and down." Simon must jump up and down as well.

2. The players will follow every time a command is given that begins with, "Simon says…" If that is not said at the beginning of the command, any players that do the action are out and will have to wait until the next round. You can mix up any order of commands from being Simon says to not including it to trip up the other person. The ultimate goal is to make the other person make a mistake.

3. Play until only one person is remaining. That person will be the next Simon. If you and your child are only you and you will play until your child makes a mistake and then switch off, so your child gets a turn as the leader.

4. When the game is over, ask your child how he or she feels about the experience. What was exciting about it? What was enjoyable? What would they want to repeat in the future? Did they learn anything?

Exercise 35: Mindful Nature Walk

Next, let's consider taking a mindful walk through nature. This is a bit different from the rainbow scavenger hunt. In this walk, you and your child will be wandering through a trail at a park, hiking, or somewhere else that is away from most people. You want the area to be mostly quiet. Nature sounds are fine, but you want to be away from as much human noise pollution as possible. This way, you know that you and your child will be focusing on nature as mindfully as possible.

This can help your child in many ways—you are getting out of the house, and you are up and about. You are getting your child moving while also facilitating their ability to focus on the world around them. They get to release that pent up energy while discovering the world around them, which is important for them to do. They learn best this way—it helps them begin to figure out how they can keep their focus on something for any period.

Try to make this a regular in your routine. You want to make sure that you and your child can find that time together regularly to practice this method. It can help you and your child bond, spend time together and make sure that you both feel connected and to the world around you. You do not need to do anything special here, either. Simply spend the day wandering around together, looking at the sky, the world around you, and everything else there is to see around you. You want you and your child to feel like you can focus on everything you can see.

It is important for you, the parent, to remember that you should follow your child's pace as you take your child on this walk. If they want to stop to study a flower, do not rush them—allow it to happen. If a rock catches their attention, let them look at it. They need to get this flexibility so they can naturally foster and harness their mindfulness. They will naturally focus on what interests them.

You can also encourage your child to take a nature journal with them—they would spend time drawing or recording anything that interests them that they find while they are on their way. If your child likes something, give them the time to write it down or draw it.

When you are done with your walk, spend some time talking with your child. What was their favorite part? What did they notice?

Exercise 36: Mindful Red Light, Green Light

This exercise will be another way to get your child up and move around while teaching them to be mindful. When you use this exercise, you will be making sure that you are encouraging your children to pay attention to what you are doing, saying, and watching you. In this edition of red light, green light, you will be mixing things up a bit. You will be allowed to hold up a sign with a light color or say the color's name at the traffic light. This means that your child will have to not only pay attention to watching you—they will also have to make sure that they are listening as well. You can also play with the pitch of your voice, encouraging it to be quieter or louder, making them pay attention to you.

You will first need a sign that you can flip between, which you can make quite simply. Color two circles of roughly the same size in to be your lights. One will be red, and the other will be green. You will want to cut them out and then take a Popsicle stick or some other sort of handle to use and paste your circles to the handle. This will be your stoplight—you will be able to simply spin it around in your hands to change your light color.

To play, take your children outside. You will need to mark a starting line and a finish line. It should be somewhat distant—you do not want your children to get there immediately.

1. Set your children at the starting line and make sure they know that they are on a red light. Have them wait and then flip the light to green. If anyone does

not leave the starting line within a second or two of you flipping the light, they lose.

2. Switch between saying red light or green light or flipping the sticks in your hands for your children to see. Any time someone fails to heed the lights, they are disqualified for the round.

3. The winner will be the person that either gets to the end of the line first or the last person standing. They will be the next sign holder.

You can also mix it up by telling your children to skip to the finish line, spin to the finish line, or do just about anything else to get there. All that matters is that your children will be paying closer attention to you while they play to focus on their surroundings.

Exercise 37: Freeze Dance

Freeze dance is another great way to get your children up on their feet and moving around to burn out that excess energy that they always seem to have while also encouraging mindfulness due to them having to listen. When you play this game with your children, you will teach them to do mindful listening. It is hard to make sure that they stop when the music stops because it is so much fun to keep up with the wiggling and running around. Because of that, it can be incredibly difficult to convince your child to stop when they need to truly. This will help them develop that awareness and willpower to pay attention to the world around them just as much as to the world within them. They will learn how they can make it a point to play the game in a meaningful way and practices those skills.

1. Choose some music that is fun to listen to and will make your children feel compelled to get up, of their feet, and dancing. This can be just about anything—all that matters is that they are having fun with it as they do it. When you go through the excitement of dancing with them, they can have even more fun.
2. Let your children get lost in the music for a while and spontaneously turn it off when your children least expect it. When the music stops, your children have to stop as well. Any children that do not stop when the music stops are out for the rest of that round.
3. Just as with the other games, the last child standing is the winner. The winner gets to pick out the next song and control the start and stop button.
4. Play this until your children look too tired to continue. When they are done, ask how they feel and what they noticed while they were playing.

You can add extra rules to the game as well—you could, for example, tell children to freeze standing on one foot when the music turns off. You could tell your children that they have to sit down when the music turns off. You could mess with the music volume to see if they are really paying attention or if they just stop when they hear the music quiet down. While you are not trying to trick your child maliciously, the game is all about messing people up to disqualify them. Get creative. Tell your children to keep working on it and help them play. Give all players a high five when the game is done and tell them what you noticed that they were doing and how well they did when they did it.

Exercise 38: Shark Fin Breathing

With all of the love for sharks among the younger generation these days, this is bound to be a great one for your children to enjoy. If your children love sharks, you can try using the shark fin breathing to help themselves. You will be encouraging your children to relax when you use these methods. You want them to make sure that they are ultimately able to pay attention to how they feel, encourage them to relax, and make sure that they use deep breathing to help themselves center themselves and relax. If you can encourage this, you will find that your children are thrilled to follow your lead.

This exercise is known as shark fin breathing because you will have them breathe with their hands in front of their faces like a shark fin poking out of the water. This is meant to be used to calm down from periods of stress.

1. Begin by encouraging your child to sit down somewhere nice and quiet. They should be relaxed and at ease while they sit, and you want them to feel encouraged to work on this method. Have them sit with their hands flat and in front of their faces. You want them to place their hands in front of them, pointing up and down, and rest it against their noses.
2. With their hands there, you want to encourage them to raise their hand toward the sky, like a shark swimming up and close their eyes. They need to move their hands down like the shark is diving back down into the water. When your child's hand is going down, they need to make an "Shhh" sound to remind themselves to quiet down and relax.

The more your child uses this exercise, the more centered he learns to become. He or she will be able to self-regulate with this, with gentle self-reminders that ultimately, they can control themselves if they choose to do so—and they should choose to do so to make sure that they do not do something in anger that they will regret.

Exercise 39: Breathing in Colors

This next exercise is going to require some degree of imagination and visualization. It will require you to guide your child into determining what their feelings would be in colors—which is quite personal, and there is no right or wrong answer—so those colors can be inhaled and exhaled. You will be essentially guiding your child's visualization, using it like a guided meditation for your child.

Start by sitting down with your child and talking about his or her feelings. How are they feeling at the moment? What color would they say that would be? How do they want to feel right now? What color do they think that would be as well? You want your child to identify these to make sure that they welcome the feelings they want without the drag down of the emotions being felt at the moment. If you do this right, you will find that your child will be much more likely to relax. After you have done all of that conversing with your child, you should be able to begin the exercise with the following steps:

1. Tell your child to sit down somewhere that is comfortable for themselves. Anywhere works—they just need to be willing to remain there for some time when they are eventually comfortable.

2. With your child comfortable, encourage him or her to relax. They should breathe deeply, but naturally. There is no changing it right now. Tell them to breathe in and out for a moment and then have them relax. Ask them to imagine the color that they are feeling right now, filling them up. Imagine it in their lungs and on their breaths.

3. Then, encourage your child to breathe out and imagine that they breathe out all of that emotion and make more room for the positive ones they want to feel. Have them release all of their negativity at this point, imagining that they are breathing out the color as well to release it into the world with their exhale.

4. Encourage your child to then breathe in the color that they wanted to feel instead. As they do, imagine that the color they want to breathe in is spreading throughout their whole body from the lungs all the way out to everywhere else.

Exercise 40: Sun Salutation Yoga Pose

This exercise is all about getting your child moving to encourage mindfulness. When they are using yoga poses to move within, they are stretching their bodies. They are encouraging deep, steady breathing. They are reminding themselves that they need to relax, and they are moving with purpose. More so, they are focused at the moment, feeling how the movement feels within them. They are seeing how the movements work for them. They are noticing how they stretch and bend, how they can move with ease.

This yoga pose that will be used is the sun salutation. It is all about spreading out and stretching. Now, you may find that for this one, you want to look up a guide online to see every step depicted in front of you.

1. Stand up tall and high. Spread your feet hip-width apart and let your feet point forward. Your arms should be next to your sides. Take a bit deep breath and then lift your hands to the sky.
2. Take a big deep exhale and bend forward. Reach down to your toes and try to touch the ground.
3. Now, place your hands down flat on the ground. Take a big, deep breath in and push one foot back behind you. You want to make sure that your back is straight while you do this, kind of like a ramp for a car.
4. Breathe out and move your other foot back to join the other one. Straighten out to make an upside-down V shape with your body. Let your neck relax. Look between your legs. What do you see? Take a breath. And another. And another. And another.

5. Breathe in and let your knees fall to the ground, like a baby crawling around on the ground. Stay here for a moment.
6. Now breathe out and sit back on your heels. Let your arms be flat at your sides and let your headrest on the mat in front of you. Pretend to be a rock.

Exercise 41: Feet Up Pose

This exercise is all about getting your feet up on the wall—literally. When you use this method, you will be encouraging your child to stop and relax for a few moments in a position that is a bit unorthodox, potentially even for your child. This particular pose is one that does not require much at all—you just need to let your legs rest flat against a wall or other flat surface and sit. This will allow your child's body to relax when he or she does it—it will enable for a flip of the circulatory system, and suddenly, the head is going to be underneath the feet. This can allow your children to relax and reset, so to speak—they will be able to sit back to refresh themselves with this, and they do not have to do very much at all.

The next time that your child is angry try guiding them through this method. It is just silly enough that it might help distract them from their anger in the first place, but it will also gently relax and refresh the body as well.

1. Encourage your child to sit back on the ground next to a wall. They need to lay down on the floor. You can use a flat pillow or a slightly folded up blanket underneath their heads so the ground does not hurt them or feel uncomfortable for them.

2. Your child must sit with their bottom against the wall, but their back should be on the floor. Think about how children will sit against a tree with their feet stretched out and their backs straight into an L shape—you are encouraging that, but with the body on the ground and the legs up on the wall instead.

3. Remain in this position for a few minutes, breathing deeply. Encourage your child to stay as long as they can, relaxing as they do so. This can help your child begin to feel better and help your child ensure that they can help themselves. You are giving your child a powerful self-soothing tool that can be used again in the future.

Exercise 42: Mindful Swinging

Most children love swinging—what is not to love? It is fun to go up toward the sky, only to swing back down to earth, and then go up again on the other side. Children love it for a good reason. It is exciting and powerful. It can be soothing and relaxing. This particular exercise is going to tap into that natural love of motion and moving around. It is honing in on the fact that children love to move around.

When you practice swinging mindfully with your child, you encourage them to feel the wind through their hair—you want them to focus on what the world around them is making them feel and why it matters. What is it that they can do in this position? What is it that they like about it? How can they focus entirely on the moment?

The nice thing about swinging is that children already naturally focus on the sensation when they are swinging. They are naturally in tune with how it makes them feel and how much they love it—that is what the draw to swinging is in the first place. Now, you are going to be piggy-backing off of that. You will be using that natural draw to swinging to encourage and foster a discussion later on.

All you need to do is go swinging with your children for a few minutes. Encourage at least one minute of quiet, mindful swinging. Encourage your child not to speak during it—tell them to focus entirely on the sensation as they do so. They should feel the wind, the stretching of their legs as they swing them in and out, and how they hold on to the chain to keep themselves from falling off.

After the minute or so of swinging is up, encourage your child to stop and talk to you about it. Ask them how it made them feel and why they felt the way that they did. Ask them to describe their feelings and sensations. Ask them if they noticed anything different when they were swinging mindfully.

Exercise 43: Watching Ripples

This next exercise will take you out to explore watching ripples as they move out and around something. You can do this in a sink full of water, a bowl, or even a lake. All you need to do is make sure that you are somewhere with a flat, mostly still body of water. If you do this in a bowl on your table, so be it, but you may be able to link this up with a mindful walk to the lake or some time traveling to a pond nearby. When you use this exercise, you will be making it a point to guide your child's focus to something that he or she may never have considered before—ripples.

Now, children generally love to throw things into the water to watch the splashes, but as soon as that first splash ends, they're right on to the next one. In this instance, however, you guide them to watch the ripples to see what happens next. You want them to see how the water continues to move and just how far away it gets before the water gets still again.

1. Set up with your body of water, wherever it may be. Gather many different items around you. Perhaps you take a few different sizes of rocks, some sticks, some leaves, and other small items to see how they will impact the water.

2. Toss in a single rock into the water. Guide your child through watching the waves splash around in the water until it falls still. What happened? Were they big waves or small waves? How far out did they stretch? Do you think that you could do it again if you tried? Guide your child through all of this—it will help them figure out what they are doing.

3. Now, choose another object to throw into the water. Watch the ripples until they end. What happens now? What if you throw some leaves into the water? What do they do?

4. Mix things up—you can also try dropping two rocks in at the same time to see what happens with your child. Ask them to guess what will happen before you do something and discuss whether they were right. This mindfulness will help them focus on the world around them and how even small actions can have a ripple effect throughout the world.

Exercise 44: Blowing Bubbles in Milk

This next exercise can get messy, so skip it if you do not want to deal with much cleanup. If you do not mind, you may want to consider laying out towels across the table before you begin for easy cleaning. This method will involve encouraging your child to do something fun—blowing bubbles—but watching closely to recognize when they have gone too far. All you need to do this is a glass of milk, which holds bubbles well quite naturally, and a straw. Towels are a recommendation but not a requirement.

You will guide your child through how hard they can blow into their milk before they make it bubble over—you explain to them that they do not want to spill the milk at all. They can blow into it, but they do not want to make any sort of a mess at the end of the day. When you encourage this from your children, they should be willing to follow along.

1. Set your child up with their cup of milk. You can make this fun and flavor the milk if you want to, or you could add food coloring to it as well. Ultimately, you will want to make sure to use real cow's milk for this exercise, so if your child does not tolerate it well, you may want to skip this one.
2. Instruct your child to blow bubbles into the milk in their cup gently. What happens when they do? How does it bubble up? Remind them that no milk is supposed to spill out of the cup when they do this, and then let them go at it.
3. Watch and see who can get their bubbles to go higher without overflowing out of the cup. If someone does make a mess or spills, they are disqualified from the contest.

4. Talk to your child at the end about how they had to change up how they were blowing as they played. Ask them what happened when they blew harder and what happened when they blew slower.

Exercise 45: Mindful Cooking

This next exercise is one that will not require you to do anything out of the ordinary—all you have to do is invite your child to cook with you. Now, you may be balking at the idea of your child in the kitchen, but rest assured—your child will be fine. Your child will learn how to cook eventually, so you may as well introduce them early. Even if your child tends to be clumsy or otherwise struggles with coordination or impulse control, you will be able to find a job for him or her in your kitchen that is safe—even if you have to think creatively about it. Even young children can be guided by helping you know what you want and guiding them. In particular, you can have young children wash vegetables if you have a stool. They can cut soft foods with a butter knife or a knife designed for children. They can throw things in the garbage or add ingredients that are not likely to splatter anywhere.

The catch here is that you have to be mindful as you do so. When you add in mindful cooking, you will be reminding your children to pay attention. You will be asking about the textures and smells. You will ask them how the dough you are rolling out feels or how those fresh herbs smell when they start to cook. You will be introducing them to tasting foods and describing the flavors, and making sure that your child knows what he or she is talking about.

This does not have to be difficult or even risky—you can even try getting cookbooks designed for children if you are concerned about contamination, dangers, or anything else. The important part here is to encourage and facilitate conversation between yourself and your child about what you are cooking and why that matters so much in the first place. Do not forget to ask your child what you feel when you have finished cooking and ask them to taste and describe their final product. This will not only add mindfulness to your daily routine, but it will also get your child involved in learning good life skills while also facilitating a conversation with them.

Exercise 46: Wall Pushes

Sometimes, it is impossible to move on past the strong emotions you feel, especially when you are young. Those feelings can be incredibly convincing and persistent. For children, in particular, those feelings can lead to problems. Children in the throes of anger may decide to throw a punch. They may hit someone. They may break something. That is not an okay behavior, and yet it happens. When it does, you may be wondering what you can do in the first place to prevent it, and for that, you can try adding in mindful wall pushes.

This exercise is going to encourage your child to stop for a moment in their anger. Your child will be pushing against the wall, moving their whole body in and out, as if doing pushups against the wall. You will encourage your child to do this instead, focusing on how it makes the body feel and asks them to pay attention to it. Remind them that ultimately, they will need to pay close attention to how they are feeling during this. Ask them to focus on their muscles as they push away from the wall and let themselves get closer.

If this works for your child, you should discover that your child is much more likely to begin to use this to calm down. This is a constructive method that your child can use to make sure that they are constructively filtering their anger. Though these exercises may look easy, they still require the use of muscles in the arms. They still put extra weight and strain on the muscles of the arms when you use it, and because of that, this can be a great way for you to make good use of your strength and energy to avoid fighting.

When your child is angry, you can ask them to go and do ten wall pushes. They may find that, when they are done, they feel better. All they have to do is inhale when they go into the wall while exhaling as they move away from the wall.

Exercise 47: Breathing and Tracing

This next exercise is all about learning how to breathe in different shapes. You may encourage your child to breathe while tracing a circle, or a square, as we saw earlier. You may have them trace the breathing exercises that they did earlier if they have done one. However, when you use this method, you will be reminding your child that ultimately, what they need to do is pay attention to their breathing as much as they can. You will teach them to mindfully follow their fingers while they breathe in and out to calm down when stressed.

You will want to sit down with your child and make all sorts of shapes on a piece of paper. Then, you will encourage your child to breathe in and out as they go over the lines. It is quite simple, and you can use it as a teaching method as well—remind your child that each shape has a name and have your child name it before tracing over it. If you do so right, your children should pick up on the shapes while also remembering to breathe.

If you do not have any shapes or paper available, you can have your child trace just about anything. Have them go over the edges of furniture or their car seat. Ask them to trace over their hand or their shirt. They can get the full use of any of these exercises just by making it a point to breathe regularly as they trace the object.

Exercise 48: Feather Catching Game

Children love feathers. There is something about them that is simply appealing, especially for young kids. Maybe it is the fact that they seem to defy gravity when they slowly and gently lilt back to the earth when they are tossed into the air. Maybe it is the fact that birds use them to fly away. Maybe it is how they look—they can be quite stunning to see in real life and up close. It could even be because they are so soft and versatile. No matter why your child loves feathers, however, you can use them through this game.

All you will need here are feathers and your child or children. Your job here is to give each child a feather and ask them to keep it in the air as long as possible while blowing at it. This will work best with small, downy feathers rather than larger ones. However, if you can do it right, you will send the flowers up into the air and watch as your children focus entirely on the feathers, desperately trying to blow them higher and higher into the air continually. If they do it right, they will be able to keep their feathers in the air for quite a while.

This requires all sorts of focus and attention, which is why it is included here—when your child is focused on the feather, they are trying desperately to keep it in the air. They have to watch the feather. They have to pay attention to the breath in their lungs. They have to blow just right when it has to happen to ensure that their feather does not hit the ground. Your child will have to pay close attention to everything—but they will have a lot of fun doing so in the first place, and that is what makes this one work so well when it comes to teaching mindfulness. When they are having fun, it will become easy, and they are honing those skills passively without even realizing it. You are teaching them to be focused and attentive. You are teaching perception and regulation. All of that will help them in the future.

Exercise 49: Follow the Maze

Children love mazes. If you go looking around at Halloween, you will see all sorts of people wandering around in corn mazes. They love them—they are fun and exciting. However, they are not always practical to grow or keep. What you can do, however, is create chalk mazes on your driveway if you have the space to do so. For this exercise, you will want to make sure that you set yourself and your child up with some chalk and plenty of space. You will draw a silly shape or maze across the cement on the ground, and your child will have to follow along with it.

You can make this quite complex, or it can be very simple. It can be endless and loop within itself, or it can have very clear beginnings and ends. Anything goes here depending upon how excited your child is to play this game and how willing and able you are to create. Set up your maze and get your child. Tell him or her that the goal here is to get throughout the entire maze but that there is no rush to do so quickly. It is not a race—they are simply following along the map's surface and seeing where it winds up. If they can do this, they should be able to foster that mindfulness by default—they will be focused on the lines, trying not to get distracted if those lines happen to pass around each other or directly intersect ever.

You can add an extra layer of mindfulness to this exercise as well if you want to make it particularly relaxing—try encouraging your child to follow along the maze while also doing the bee breathing exercise. Tell your child that they pretend to be a bee doing their dance to figure out where the flowers with nectar and pollen are. Your child may get a kick out of the guided visualization, and it may further encourage them in their actions.

Exercise 50: Mindful Gardening

The last exercise we are going to entertain within this chapter is mindful gardening. Now, you may be dubious that your child will even like gardening in the first place—

but children love dirt and getting outside. You may doubt that you have much space—but even a single small spot on your windowsill could be enough if you are truly that short on space. There are ways around your constraints. If neither of those options works for you, you may be able to find a community garden as well that will have space for your child to plant something.

Spend some time with your child, trying to find something that you know will grow well in your area. This will be very climate-dependent, but you should find something that will work well for you. Identify that plant for you and ensure that you do your research about their gardening requirements. Remember that different plants will need different lighting requirements, fertilization, and even different amounts of space. You will need to consider this all with your child—this can be an exercise in mindfulness itself, encouraging your child to research with you.

Gather up all of your supplies. You should have your pots, your soil, your seeds or sprouts, and anything else that you think you will need. Allow your child to dig the holes to plant the plants slowly. Encourage your child to do anything that is age-appropriate during this time and make sure that they can pick up what they want to do while also figuring out exactly how to make it work for them.

From there, you will want to make it a routine for your child—they will need to stop and water their plants daily. They will need to make sure that they are always pulling out any weeds or leaves that do not look healthy. Guide your child through the process, making sure that the plants are getting everything that they need, but make sure that ultimately, your child is the one that is responsible. They will be the ones getting the benefit.

By quietly and carefully going through the gardening process and encouraging and facilitating your plants' repeated care, you will be teaching your child about responsibility and regulation. In essence, they will have to self-regulate to make sure that the plants are ultimately taken care of, which can be tough. Do not hesitate to offer reminders in the early days, but also remember that your child needs to develop that sense of responsibility.

Chapter 5: Mindful Exercises for Trauma and Anxiety

Exercise 51: The Glitter Jar

Children love glitter, and quite frankly, what's not to love? It is pretty to look at. It sparkles. It can be quite colorful. It can get on anything, and it will be one of the last objects still on Earth if there were ever to be the destruction of humanity. It would be right there alongside the cockroaches—surviving for eternity in cracks and fissures, remnants from craft projects that happened years prior.

All jokes aside about how glitter is almost permanently a part of your life as soon as it gets welcomed in the first place, we will be looking at creating glitter jars in this chapter. Glitter jars are jars filled up with water and glitter that can be shaken up kind of like a snow globe. The glitter will shake around and slowly settle back down to the bottom, and your child can use this to be a sort of mindful regulator for themselves if they need that extra push for themselves. We will look at how to make these and then use them as a time out timer to remind your child to relax.

All you will need is a jar of some sort, glitter that will sink, glitter glue, food coloring, and food coloring if you want it. You will be mixing this to create the jar, and then, you will be able to use this jar for your child to shake up to watch settle. You can use this jar to talk about feelings—about how any anxiety or fears are just like that glitter, shaking up inside, but they can also all fall back down to the ground as well if you let them.

1. Start by taking your jar. Fill it up about 1/3 of the way with glitter glue. Then, about half of a jar's worth of water to the mix. Finally, top off with as much glitter as you want inside of it. Remember that ultimately, you need a bit of a gap at the top of the jar so it can be shaken around, but you can determine just how much glitter you want. Put in any drops of food coloring if you want it to have a color. Seal up the jar and give it to your child.
2. Your child can now shake up the jar as much as possible. That first time it is used, you will need to shake it long enough to dissolve all of its glue. The glue should not be visible separately from the water. It is okay if you can see the glitter itself—and that is preferable, but the glue itself should be gone.
3. Your child feels strong emotions that cannot be controlled, encouraging them to shake their jar up. Have them sit and watch until all of the glitters settles down to the bottom of the jar before continuing to talk about their feelings.

When you do this, you may want to keep in mind that you may want to use a plastic jug rather than a glass jar for younger children. You can also influence just how long it will take for the glitter to settle down by making sure that you add more or less glitter to the jar by age. You may only use the glitter glue with a small amount of excess glitter for a very young child. For older children, you may add more.

Exercise 52: Five Senses Grounding Exercise

This next exercise is all about grounding oneself. If your child finds that he or she gets stressed out frequently or feels like he or she is out of control, this is a good exercise to have in their back pocket even when trying to manage themselves. This is all about using their senses to help themselves self-regulate, and if you play your cards right, you can teach your child to make sure that, even when emotions are running high, they can simply focus on the senses to help themselves begin to relax.

In particular, you will want to use this when your child is calmer, making it into a sort of I-spy game at first. This can help your child get used to the process. However, they can also use it to calm themselves down. This requires engagement from all five senses, much like how they were engaged earlier in one of the worksheets provided to you. Try using this by reading the following prompts to your child.

1. First, you must find five things that you can see. What do you see all around you? [You can then add in questions about what there is around you. If your child is particularly troubled, you can try listing out several things around you that you can see as you can see them. This will help your child begin to find their center.]

2. Now, you need to find four things that you can hear. I can hear [insert what you can hear here. You can add all sorts of different things here. Ask your child about what they hear and what it sounds like to get

them thinking about what is around them and how it influences them.]

3. Next, you need to find three things that you can touch. What are you touching right now? [You can now ask questions about what your child is in contact with. It may be bare feet on the grass, or it could be the feeling of a sweater against his or her skin. No matter what it is, encourage your child to focus on it.]

4. Now, it is two things that you can smell. What is that smell nearby? [You would then ask questions about what your child can smell around you and what that means for them. This can be silly, or it can be serious, depending upon your child's current state and what your end goal is. If you are trying to alleviate fear, you may use something funny, but if you want your child to relax and fall asleep, you may be a bit more serious about it.]

5. Finally, you need to tell me one thing that you can taste right now. What does the inside of your mouth taste like?

Allow your child to use this method as much or as little as makes sense for them. However, keep in mind that this can be a great way to return to a base neutral state when anxious or afraid.

Exercise 53: Roots to Rising Meditation

This next exercise is a bit of a guided meditation more than anything else. You will be guiding your child through a meditation in which your child focuses on their feet and up into the sky. You will be working on your child with a mindful focus on the yoga done in this particular exercise. You want your child to root, meaning they are firm and strong. They are learning to plant themselves where they are. When they rise, they are allowing themselves to be kind and caring to everyone around them. However, you cannot rise steadily without first rooting. Just like a plant needs to have solid roots to stand and grow, your child will need to learn how to plant his or her roots as well.

1. Start by standing with feet apart. Imagine them rooting into the ground. Feel the energy going from the feet into the ground. Place your palms out and stretch out your back. Breathe in deeply, feeling the breath from the feet and slowly moving up the body. Imagine the oxygen moving up higher and higher until it reaches the head. Now, breathe out. Repeat this three times.
2. Now, breathe in and reach out as widely as you can—stretch out your fingers and lift your arms, so they are above your head. They should touch above you like you are clapping. When you breathe out now, you should take your arms away from each other and then bend down to touch the ground. Put your hands on the ground and pat it. Feel the strength in the ground in you.
3. Now, rise as much as you can, pulling the ground's strength with you. Imagine it in your hands and let it hold your head and arms heavily as you slowly stretch up to one bite at a time. Slowly, slowly stand up, and when you are up all the way, put your

hands back up above your head and put your hands together. Then, pull your hands back down to your heart and say, "I'm strong and firm."

4. Repeat the previous steps, but with every new iteration, change the affirmation used. Perhaps one time, you tell yourself that you are strong. One time you say that you are brave. Another time you say kind or beautiful, or peaceful.

This should allow your child to think about themselves. They can think about how strong they are and why they really, truly matter in the world. When you use these methods with your child, they will learn to respect themselves and where they stand. They will feel better, and they can use this to chase off the fear and doubt that anxiety commonly brings with it.

Exercise 54: Gratitude Game

This next game is meant to help your child think of things that they are grateful for. Gratefulness is a major component of mindfulness just because they are so closely related—they both require an acceptance of what is happening right at that moment, no matter whether it is good or bad. This means that when you teach your child to be grateful, you remind your child that ultimately, he or she needs to be paying attention to the world. You are entering your child's thoughts into positivity and gratefulness, and that is important.

When you play the gratefulness game, you look around at what you have in your general vicinity and discuss what you are grateful for. It is that simple—the entire purpose is to facilitate conversation about what you and your child are grateful for and why it matters so much. When you use this, you allow your child to hear you speaking kindly about the world and what you have in it. You are teaching your child that, ultimately, they have enough in the world, and because they have just enough, they have no reason to worry about getting more. Your child learns that ultimately, what they need to do is accept what they have rather than demanding more selfishly.

Every day before your child goes off to bed, ask your child to name three things that he or she was grateful for that day. This is the best way to begin that process of talking about what they are grateful for while also beginning to foster that understanding of what matters the most in life. When you use this, you are teaching your child to pay attention to the world around them. You are guiding your child through how to recognize what they appreciate the most.

You can add to this by asking your child what they are thankful for when something goes wrong. While most children will understandably be annoyed or frustrated when something goes wrong, you can still spend the time to ask them what matters the most to them at the end of the day. Ask them to point out what it is that they got that motivates them to move forward. Ask them why that matters. Ask them what they can be glad about. And most importantly, make sure that it is a dialogue and that you are listening.

Exercise 55: Mindful Visualization

Another great way to help with any anxiety is through using mindful visualization. This is quite simple to employ in your life—all it will require is that you take the time to ensure that you regularly involve yourself. You could read stories to your child without pictures, encouraging them to listen and follow along in their minds. You can find many of these precisely for mindful visualization before bed to help your child relax and unwind. You can find many other scripts online that you can utilize if you are unsure where to begin.

Another way that you can do this is through the use of videos. There are many different recordings of people reading over these sorts of mindful guides you can take advantage of. When you use mindful visualization with your child, all that matters is that they have that visualization aid in the first place, whether it is in your voice or not. So long as they have it, they can practice the process.

These exist about just about anything. You can find bedtime stories about dragons and princes. You can find them about learning meditative techniques to help your child get further in life and rein in their anxiety. You can find them about learning to be assertive or those that are going to teach your child that they ultimately matter just as much as everyone else around them. No matter what you and your children choose to use, remember that the tool is greatly useful.

The best time to use these meditations will be at night before bed or first thing in the morning. Find some recordings if you can, or make them a gentle part of your bedtime routine to encourage yourself and your child to relax. You will likely find that you see a drastic difference in how your child behaves and what you can expect from them.

Exercise 56: Partner Breathing

This next exercise is known as partner breathing. It requires two people to make it work, as you would guess by looking at the title. This exercise is a great one to make use of. You may find that you will do this with your child, or you can have two of your children work together here, depending upon what you need. This is a comfortable way to get your children looking at other people as well—it teaches your children empathy and how to focus on other people as well.

You will guide your child with the following script:

1. Start by sitting up tall. Make sure your back is touching your partner as much as it can. You can have your legs; however, you want to be as comfortable as you can be.
2. Take in a few deep breaths and feel your partner's back behind you, supporting you. You can feel your partner breathing too. Close your eyes and bring your own hands to your own heart and belly.
3. Take a few big, deep breaths, nice and slowly. Can you feel your partner's breathing too? Think about how your partner is breathing right now. Feel it yourself as you do so. Are they breathing long or short? Is it deep or shallow? Is it smooth or kind of bumpy? Think about their breaths and focus on it as much as you can for as long as you can.
4. Stay this way for a while, and see what happens. Just listen and feel your partner's breaths. What does it sound like?
5. Do you feel your breathing synchronizing up with your partner's? Are your breathing rates becoming the same? Why? Why not?

6. Focus on your partner's breathing and match pace. How does it feel? Focus on how connected you and your partner are and feel that bond. Stay here as long as you would like to.

When you encourage this sort of empathy with each other, you teach your child that they ultimately do have that power to tap into other people. They can relate to other people. Your child and anyone else has the same basic needs—you need to breathe together. You need love. You need food and water. All animals need to breathe, and recognizing that can help bring that sort of mindful connection to the forefront of your child's mind.

Exercise 57: Mindful Barefoot Walking

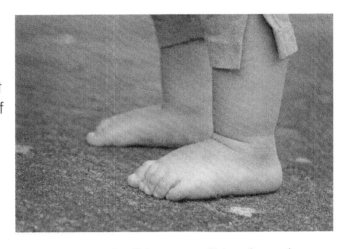

This next exercise is going to be one that is best done outside, if possible. You and your child are going to be exploring the world through barefoot walking. When you do this, you will be focusing entirely on your feet, planting you on the ground, as will your child. You will be able to teach your child that they can feel the ground supporting them and that they always have that to fall back on—literally. The ground is always there as constant support that will not be going anywhere, and that is a sort of constant that they can latch onto when they are anxious.

When you do this exercise, you and your child will be wandering barefoot. Make sure that the area that you choose out is one that is safe for this—you want to make sure that you are not at risk for being bitten by anything, for example, and you want to make sure that the area is free and clear of sharp rocks, glass, or anything else that could potentially hurt you or your child. When you remove those dangers, you know that your child is much more likely to be safe, and therefore, you can relax a bit about having them walking barefoot in the first place.

1. Take off your shoes and socks. Put them away. Now, what do you feel under your feet? What is that between your toes? Do you feel the earth there? Is the grass tickling between your toes? Is the ground warm or cold? Is it soft or hard? Encourage your child to stop and think about the ground as they walk around on it without shoes. Encourage them to take a few steps around as well—what is out there? How does the ground change from step to step?

2. Try walking around different grounds as well. What does it feel like to walk on sand? On gravel? In soft grass? In dirt? You can encourage this in several different instances, but each time you want to return to is asking just how much your child can focus on the ground and what that ground makes him or her feel. What do they like about it? What don't they like about it? Would they rather wear shoes? Can they feel mud under their feet? Are they sinking deeper, or are they solidly on top?

This process is meant to help your child learn to identify their surroundings with their feet and facilitate the ability to focus on the ground and how they can be planted within it. When you use this method, you are encouraging your child to feel that connection and to be able to focus on where they stand in the world.

Exercise 58: Superhero Senses

Every child imagines being a superhero at some point—but how many of them can make it happen? Encourage your child here to stop and use their senses to focus on the world around him or her. They can do this quite easily—they have their superpower if they learn how to tap into it. They can tap into that ability to focus on the world around them compellingly and identify far more than they ever thought possible.

You can start this process by encouraging your child to be as attentive as possible. Ask your child what superheroes need to be able to do: They need to be able to find bad guys. You can ask your child, then, what do those superheroes need to make it happen? They may announce that the superheroes need super hearing or super smelling or super sight. Those are all fair points. Remind your child that they can have that super sense as well—with mindfulness and focusing on the world.

You can guide your child by closing their eyes and focusing on the world. You will guide your child through trying to quiet their mind, encouraging them to stop thinking and just listen. Ask them if they can hear the target—perhaps you are looking for your dog or cat. Guide them through mindfully hunting down their pet as easy as possible to see if they can find them with their senses.

Then, remind your child that they can use these senses and abilities at any time. If they get lost from the group, they can listen closely to find their friends by voice. If they lose sight of someone, they can focus on just one feature of that person to hunt down instead of looking for the whole person. When they begin to use their senses more efficiently, they will be much more capable of tapping into what they need around them.

Exercise 59: Mindful Scavenger Hunt

This next activity will require mindfulness to find items that will be predetermined. You may decide to hide the items that you are going to expect your child to find, sort of like an Easter egg hunt, or you may just make a list full of clues and expect your child to figure out how to find everything that they are looking for. No matter the method you chose, your child will be sent off to find different items, and the focus that they will need will come from that very same mindfulness discussed thus far.

Start by figuring out your setting that you will want to use for the hunt. Are you doing it at home? In your yard? At a park? On a hike? Identify that location first, so you know what to expect in terms of what can be hidden or what can be found in the first place. For the best effect, you can do this along with a mindful nature walk as well, deciding to come up with a scavenger hunt list of items to find all around them.

With your setting identified, make up a list of clues for your child. Younger children may get a list of items to find while older children may get a riddle that they have to solve before they know what they are looking for.

Print off the list and then take your children to the proper location for the hunt. Give them the lists and then tell them that they have to find everything on the list to win some sort of prize that you have determined. Go through the walk and watch as they hunt all around them to find the items they are looking for. Keep in mind that if you are taking your children into a natural setting, you are not guaranteed to find anything at all if it is alive and, therefore, can move around. You may decide that you keep your clues relatively vague to allow for as much wiggle room as possible. For example, instead of dictating that your child must find a male duck, you may declare that they need to find a bird on the water.

Exercise 60: The Silence Game

Children talk. A lot. However, you can teach them to appreciate the sound of silence, as well. They can learn to appreciate it when nothing is happening—they can learn to recognize all of the sounds around them and why those sounds are unique and worthy of hearing on their own. You can teach your children that, ultimately, they want to be able to stop and enjoy the quiet every once and a while to enjoy themselves truly.

When you want your children to play the silence game, you do not tell them to be quiet just to get your own few minutes of silence. Rather, you are telling them to be quiet so *they* can appreciate it. Ask them to spend a certain amount of time perfectly quiet. Remember to be realistic about this—if your child is young, make sure that you ultimately do not take longer than a minute or two to try to get them to be quiet. You will need to work within the constraints of their ages. Set the time and tell them to be quiet.

Have them focus on the quiet—have them notice that ultimately, even when they are not making noise, it is still quite loud all around them. Perhaps, they will notice the faint buzzing of the fan is suddenly quite loud. The dog next door is barking, and they can hear it. They can even hear the sounds of their breathing or the sizzling of the food in the kitchen. You are teaching them that when they stop and remain still, even for a moment, they will discover so much more in the world around them, and that is beautiful. You are reminding them that ultimately when they do fall quiet for some time, they will be able to explore this as well, and you can teach them to appreciate the sound of silence.

Exercise 61: Anchoring

We are now going to explore another yoga exercise—this one is the anchor breath. When you use this method, you guide your child to focus his or her mind on one particular point. Generally speaking, you will want to do this somewhere that your child will be aware of and somewhere that breathing will be influenced. Your child will place their hand somewhere on their body, and that point of contact will be their anchor point that they will be focusing on. You can encourage your child to do this on their stomachs, chests, or noses. It does not matter where so long as it moves when they breathe.

You will encourage your child to do the following:

1. Place your hands on top of each other, either on your heart, on your tummy, or in front of your nose. It is up to you to choose which spot you prefer.

2. Breathe in deeply as you sit there for a moment. Pay attention to that one spot. This is now your anchor spot. Feel the sensation of breathing underneath your hands. Feel your hands rise higher and higher with that inhale, and then exhale, too. Focus on that feeling.

3. Encourage your child to continue to breathe for some time—they may last for a minute, or they may last for five. However, no matter how long or short, allow them to continue the process as long as possible to appreciate the breathing practice.

4. Any time your mind starts to wander, return it to your hands and your breathing. Stay here as long as you can.

This will guide your child through this process of mindfulness, focusing entirely on breathing and ensuring that your child is well aware of what his or her body is doing at that moment. When your child finishes up, ask them how they feel about it. Ask if they feel refreshed. Ask what they noticed about the process and what stood out to them.

Exercise 62: Coloring Your Feelings

Next, we are going to address another art project for your child to do mindfully. This project will have your child assign colors to their feelings and then focus on those feelings to figure out their feelings. As they find their feelings, they can then begin to color them onto their paper. As before, you want to give your child whatever it is that they want to use for tools at this point. If they want to use crayons or markers, they can do so. If they want to use paint, allow that if you are willing. The medium is not important here—what matters is that they express themselves.

Perhaps you decide to print off a paper that will require your child to use fine motor skills to get in there and stay between the lines. Maybe you decide to simply encourage your child to color without any boundaries to focus on at all. No matter what your child chooses, all that matters here is that your child can color on the paper for an extended period, quietly and mindfully trying to convey his or her emotions onto the paper to make it present.

When your child is coloring mindfully, their focus is entirely on the paper they are coloring on. They are quietly redirecting their attention to that one point in which their coloring utensil and their paper meet, watching as they permanently change the paper into something entirely different altogether. They are creating something with their emotions, and there is something beautiful and valuable in that alone—they can begin to figure out patterns in their own emotions using this. They can begin to realize that when they are upset, they regularly color a certain way. When they are frustrated, they do something else. They may notice how their pencils move on their paper is different when they have different emotions. They may simply focus on those emotions to see what happens within themselves. Anything is valid here. All that is important is that your child is quiet and present.

Exercise 63: Reframing a Thought

This next exercise is quite practical—it is meant to help someone change their thought process from a negative one to a positive one. Often, when we look at the world, we do so with a very specific frame dependent upon our position. How we feel right now can also directly alter how we present ourselves and decide to see the world. This is important to keep in mind—it means that we can also begin to shift that frame if it changes so much.

With this exercise, you will encourage your child to change that frame of mind by looking at something. You are encouraging them to take a new perspective. You are guiding them through trying to figure out what matters the most to them. You are encouraging them to change up what they are doing and how they will do it. You remind them that they can ultimately control their thoughts if they are willing and able to take that power into their own hands.

The easiest way to do this is to create a sort of negativity challenge. When your child has a negative thought, immediately counter it. Your child has to voice three positive thoughts about the same situation for every negative thought to find the best in what is happening. Things can be quite negative, but there is almost always some degree of positivity that can be found in just about everything. Hold your child to this, and you will quickly discover it for yourself as well—they can change their thoughts to be more positive as well.

Exercise 64: Star Pose

This exercise is another yoga pose—but unlike most of the other ones, this particular pose is one in which your child does not have to do anything at all—all they have to do is a flop. As the name implies, all your child has to do is stand or lay down with their body shaped like a star. This means feet and legs are wide apart, and arms are stretched out to the sides. When your child does this standing up, they can work on balance and muscles within the core. However, when this is done while lying down, it can help re-center your child and help them cope if they have any sorts of anxiety or negativity present within themselves at that particular moment. When you use this method, you teach your child that their body is so strong that it can directly alter their thinking and feeling.

1. Begin by taking the mountain pose—this means that your feet are together, and you are standing big and tall. Your spine is nice and straight, and you are holding your hands out, palms out. Take a big, deep breath here and feel the stretch.
2. Slowly step to stretch your feet apart from each other. You want your feet to be as wide apart as possible with you remaining balanced. Stretch your arms out as far as you can to your sides, like they are airplane wings. Hold them there.
3. Breathe for a few moments, in and out, slowly and deeply. Make sure that you keep the pose while you breathe. Then, when you are ready, drop your arms down gently and step back together.

Exercise 65: Make an I Spy Jar

This next exercise can be a lot of fun to do with your child. You are going to be creating an I-Spy jar. This is drawing inspiration from the game I-spy in which you can find items that someone else has called out for you within your environment. In this particular case, however, you are filling up a jar primarily with one object, such as sand or beads, and then you are adding in a bunch of smaller items as well that can fit in there and act as the subjects for your child to find when they are using it.

All you will need here is a jar that is large enough to fit all of the items you wish to include and some sort of substance to act as the filler. Sand and rice are both easy ones that are large enough that they won't just coat over the objects and are not dark enough to obscure the object either completely. Dirt may cause you problems if it cakes all-around your items.

1. Find your supplies—choose your filler material and several small items that you can include within the jar. You may throw in a penny, a marble, a tack, some beads, a toy army man, or just about anything else that you think you could fit in there that will not go bad or get damaged.

2. Pour in a little bit of your substance and then drop in an item or two. Add a little more of the material before another item. Repeat this process throughout the jar until you are out of items and it is mostly full. Leave a little bit of space at the top—maybe a quarter of the jar or so—to allow the materials to be

shifted around or shaken up to expose what you are looking for. Close the lid as tightly as you can.

3. Shake up the jar and begin playing! If your child feels stressed or bored, you can encourage them to look through their jar to find the items within it. They will always be moving around just because the jar will shift around.

Exercise 66: Hand Full of Sand

This next exercise is meant to encourage your child to feel the sand in their hands closely and mindfully. You can do this at a park or a beach, or even  in your back yard if you have a sandbox. Wherever you are doing, it is not so important. Ultimately, you will be guiding your child to stop, feel the sand in their hands, and then breathe as they allow it to spill through their fingers. When you do this, you are encouraging your child to focus on the sensation. They are learning to pay attention to how the world around them feels as they touch it, and that is powerful.

Take your child to somewhere with sand and encourage them to take up a big handful of it. Allow them to feel it in their hands. Do they notice how it shifts and spills, almost like water? Have them pay attention to this sensation for a few moments. How does it feel as the sand slides out? Does it tickle? Is it relaxing? Do they like it? You want your child to focus on this for a few moments until they are ready to move on and look at something else instead. Encourage this as long as you can.

After a bit, try adding water to the sand as well. How does water change the texture? How does it flow when the water is added to it? Does it clump together, or does it continue to spill out? Why? How does it feel different now?

You will want to encourage your child to explore the sand with their hands and potentially their feet if they are able. The changes in textures can be a wonderful way to focus on mindfulness to stick with them. They will likely feel entirely compelled to pay attention to the textures shifting around within their hands. They will enjoy the sensation of the sand slipping, and you can enjoy watching them learn to focus.

Exercise 67: Mindful Guided Meditation

This next exercise is a guided meditation. For this, you will want to figure out what it is that you want to guide your child through in the first place. Do you want them to be guided in feeling more confident? Do you want them to be guided through how to relax or trust the world they are in? Maybe you want them to feel like they can trust themselves or how they can begin to feel good in a world that they may find it difficult to be in.

When you are using a guided meditation, you will first want to make sure that your child is old enough to follow along. For the most part, until the ages of 6 or 7, your child may struggle with a genuine meditation instead of some sort of visualization exercise, as has been discussed earlier within this book. However, if your child is old enough and you know what you would like to guide your child through learning to do, this exercise may be great for you and may give you both exactly what you will need to see.

Ultimately, there are hundreds and hundreds of meditation sources online. Because children vary so much developmentally from age to age, their meditative abilities can vary so much; you will want to look up a guided meditation for a child the age of the one you are considering using this with. Encourage them to think and encourage them to be open-minded about the process when you guide them through this. For some people, meditation is difficult. It is something they are inherently doubtful toward, and that can hold them back. Try to encourage an open mind and try finding a good guided meditation that will catch and keep your child's interest and guide them through whatever they need then.

Exercise 68: Mindful Storytime

This next exercise is sort of similar to meditation—however, rather than encouraging your child to be mindful, you are going to be encouraging your child to listen empathetically. When you use mindful storytime, you can use any story that comes to mind. It could be a fun one, a silly one, or a serious one. You can even use whatever the book your child has been reading lately is to guide this process. No matter what the story is, you ultimately want your child to be engaged in it and therefore want to make sure that it will hold your child's interest.

Read to your child for a short while. This works best if you are reading a book without pictures, so your child is not distracted. The point here is for your child to stop and listen to the words as you read them aloud. Your child should be visualizing the story in his or her head rather than just looking at pictures illustrated on the page. While the pictures will always have their own time and place, it is also important to recognize that your child's ability to visualize will take them far. It can be quite helpful in emotional regulation.

When you have finished reading the story to your child, encourage them to talk about their thoughts. How did the characters feel when something big happened? How did your child feel when they read over it? What did that make your child think or feel? Why do those thoughts or feelings happen or become relevant here? What is going to happen next? Why?

This process will encourage your child to think critically and relate to the characters. These are both incredibly important life skills, and this mindfulness, this attention to detail, and attention to the story itself are what help that happen.

Exercise 69: Validating Emotions

Your child has emotions. You probably know this better than anyone else. You have seen your child lose it over something breaking or a disappointment. You have seen your child furious when something does not go quite his or her way. This happens—children are emotional creatures. They do not yet know how to regulate themselves. If you want your child to learn how to regulate themselves in the first place, the best starting point is through taking the time to validate your child's emotions.

You may be thinking that you already do this, but you sometimes unintentionally invalidate how they feel. You may tell them that they are fine when they are crying—you are telling them that their feelings are wrong. You may tell them that there's nothing to cry about—again telling them that their emotions are wrong, out of place, or otherwise inappropriate for some reason. This is not fair to your child—you cannot hope to take over your child's emotional reactions and tell them that theirs are wrong. What if someone told you that you have no reason to be upset when someone scrapes up your car? You would probably be pretty annoyed. Your child is also annoyed and frustrated by this sort of avoidance and this sort of disregard for his or her emotions—they are very real to your child, and you need to be able to recognize and appreciate that.

You can validate your child by acknowledging what they are feeling. Put a name to their frustration. If your daughter has just come home, sobbing and telling you that she was broken up with, you are not doing her any favors by shrugging and saying that everyone gets broken up with in high school. You are invalidating those emotions. Is it true?

Mostly—the vast majority of high school relationships end. However, that does not mean that it helps your child feel any better about it.

Instead, offer sympathy. Offer empathy as well. Let your child know that you understand how they are feeling, and you get it. You need to allow them to feel their feelings. Let them experience what they are feeling without trying to disregard it or without undermining it.

Exercise 70: Sniffing Flowers and Blowing Candles

This next exercise is perfect for younger children—,, particularly around the toddler age. At younger ages, children struggle to be able to understand the instructions behind deep breathing. It can help them if you turn it into some sort of game for them. Instead of telling them to stop crying simply or to take a deep breath, you can guide them through the process with imagination. In this case, you are going to make their breathing into sniffing flowers and blowing out candles.

When you need your child to inhale, tell them to imagine that they are taking in a big, deep sniff of a flower. You can even hold your hand out like you are holding out a pretend flower for them to smell in front of you. They should stop and take in a big, deep breath when you do this. You can even make this fun by adding silly smells. "Here, sniff my watermelon flower!" or "Look, it's my candy flower! Sniff it!"

After the inhale, you want them to exhale slowly and deeply through the mouth. Try telling them to blow out candles. Children love blowing out candles—they usually associate it with blowing out birthday candles on a cake, so you can generally get all sorts of agreement with this one. Have your child take a quick blow at your hand, which you can then hold flat for them as if a candle is resting on it.

Repeat this process a few times, and you have just guided your toddler or preschooler through how to take deep breaths. In particular, you may find that this works best if your child is upset—it can help your child learn to self-regulate through breathing early on.

Exercise 71: Mountain Breath

This next breathing exercise is yet another pull from yoga—as you can guess by now, yoga is a great place to start when it comes to mindfulness. With this position, you are encouraging your child to sit or stand tall and breathe, imagining that they are as big or as tall as a mountain as they breathe. You can add an extra layer to this by telling them that their breaths are the winds that pass the mountain. This pose should be quite easy for most children, and you can use it just about anywhere with them.

1. Start by either sitting or standing up. You can choose either, so long as you keep your back straight and your head high. You are a mountain! You have to be tall like one!

2. Inhale through your nose and lift your arms all the way up past your head. Close your palms together. You are a big, tall mountain. Imagine that your hands together are the tallest peak on the mountain. You are big and strong and sturdy.

3. Breathe out through your mouth, blowing gently like the wind. Let it all out in front of you and let it all fade away. As you do this, bring your hands, still pressed together, in front of your chest.

4. Take another big, deep breath and focus on the feeling of the air in your lungs. Then, breathe it out and imagine the wind blowing elsewhere. The wind can blow all around you, but it cannot move the big, keen mountain.

You can encourage your child to remain in this position for as long as they would like, slowly and quietly breathing. They should feel better very quickly by doing this, and you may find that your child begins to use these for him or herself as well.

Exercise 72: Pouring Paint

This next exercise is quite simple—but it is messy. You may want to put down a tarp where you are using this particular method if you do not want to be scrubbing up paint or if you have young children that may spill. You could even consider doing this in the bathtub with smaller children that will still fit in there comfortably. When you use this method, you will need runny tempera paints and a small enough canvas that your child can conveniently pick up and move around.

1. Begin by pouring one of the paints onto the canvas. You can pour as much or as little onto it. It should pool on the canvas. Try not to let it spill!

2. Pour another color onto the canvas where you want it. Then choose another and another. You can make this as colorful as you would like, or you can leave it with just one or two colors if you would prefer.

3. When the canvas is mostly covered in paint, and there are large puddles on it, you can now pick up the art. Be careful to keep it straight up, or you risk spilling the paint! Now, tip it around, back and forth, side to side. The paints will start to pour around the canvas, creating new patterns without totally blending. Move the canvas as much as you would like, tilting it from side to side but careful not to lose all of the paint.

4. When you are done, set the canvas down somewhere safe to dry. Remember, with all of that paint on it; it may need a couple of days to dry fully.

Exercise 73: Positive Thoughts and Affirmations

This next exercise is about remembering to keep thoughts positive through the use of affirmations. Affirmations are little phrases that can be repeated to you in periods of stress or anger when you feel overwhelmed and cannot keep going. You may find that they get overwhelmed and then feel like they are not good enough for your child. You can then counter this by having your child repeat an affirmation—perhaps reminding her that she *is* good enough the way that she is.

When you use these exercises, you will want to help your child develop a good affirmation for him or her. This means you need to figure out their biggest insecurities or problems and target those. Remind your child that he or she is good enough, smart enough, or caring enough, and any time that you hear your child getting down about him or herself, repeat this affirmation back to them to make them feel better. Over time, they should start to absorb it.

You can also have your child repeat these affirmations every morning while brushing teeth or getting ready for bed. The more they repeat them, the more likely they are to stick and remain positive influences.

Exercise 74: Smile

This next exercise is all about smiling. Even if you don't feel like smiling, you can begin to get those benefits if you do so. You may fake the smile at first for a while, but your body and mind will synchronize up, and you will start to feel better. You can do this same thing with your child. Encourage your child to smile and then have them focus on what happens within their body when they do so. They may be surprised at how many muscles smiling requires and be shocked that it can be so exhausting.

Start by encouraging your child to smile—either make them smile by being silly or have them pretend to smile. Ask them what they feel. Ask them what they notice in their face and how it feels. Ask them where they feel the smile the most as they are smiling. Is it their cheeks? Their lips? Anywhere else? Encourage them to continue reflecting on their smiles for a moment before letting them relax and move on.

You may be surprised at the reactions that you get from your child. They may feel better after this exercise. They may be quietly focused on their face for a while after. They may realize that they feel better when they smile and start to use it more later on. However, you have taught them that smiling can be a valuable resource for themselves no matter what.

Exercise 75: Bubble Breathing

Finally, this last exercise that you are going to see is bubble breathing. This is going to require your children to focus on their breathing and how they do it. You will be guiding them by seeing the difference between deep breathing and quick breathing through blowing bubbles. You will need to gather up bubble solution, bubble wands and head outside for this exercise.

1. Get your children all set up with some bubbles. Ask them to blow some normally for a minute or two and then ask them about it. How did the breathing feel?

2. Next, ask your children to breathe normally without blowing to see what happens with their bubbles. They may find that they do not get any bubbles at all when this happens. Ask what they noticed and how they feel.

3. Then, ask them to blow their bubbles very, very quickly with quick breaths. As they do this, ask how it

makes them feel and ask if they like it. They may realize that they are feeling more energized with this method.

4. Ask them to slow down their breathing as well and see what happens. How does it change the way that the bubbles blow out? Does it get easier or harder? Do they make more or less?

When they finish the exercise, encourage them to reflect on how the different breaths changed. Point out how sometimes they had more bubbles, and other times, there were none. Ask them which breathing made them feel the best and why.

Conclusion

Congratulations! You have made it to the end of *Mindfulness and Self-Regulation for Children*. At this point, you have been guided through how you can begin to foster self-regulation in children. This is a valuable skill that children need to know—it is incredibly important for them to recognize how they can change their emotions and why it matters. When you realize that you can teach these skills to your children and learn them, you will find that life with them gets a lot less complex. They can stop throwing tantrums themselves most of the time. They can learn to self-regulate. They can reflect on their actions, and all of this will make them better people, better friends, and better partners in the future.

At this point, all that is left for you to do is to get involved. Start implementing mindfulness wherever you can. Remember, mindfulness is not something to practice here and there. It is a lifestyle—you must learn to live mindfully if you want to raise mindful children, and the best way to do so is through making sure that you are remaining diligent, focused, and attentive with your children. Pay attention to them and what they want or need. Make sure that they see you paying attention to them. Foster that connection with them and teach them to do so as well. They will pick up on what you are modeling and become much more likely to live that same life. Take your child for a walk on one. Take them out to learn yoga. Practice these breathing exercises. Play. Read stories together. You can implement mindfulness just about everywhere, and this book has given you 75 different ways that you can.

Finally, thank you so much for picking up this book to share with your children. Hopefully, the book itself was enjoyable for you—one that is memorable enough for you to continue to reference and use for years to come. You will be able to use these activities to foster a lifetime of mindfulness if you so choose. Thank you once more, and good luck as you teach these skills to your children.

If you have found this book valuable at all, please head over to Amazon to share your thoughts! Feedback, criticism, comments, and general opinions are always greatly welcomed!